Why America?

KURT HAAS

iUniverse, Inc.
New York   Bloomington

Why America?

iUniverse books may be ordered through booksellers or by contacting:

iUniverse
1663 Liberty Drive
Bloomington, IN 47403
www.iuniverse.com
1-800-Authors (1-800-288-4677)

ISBN: 978-1-4401-2237-8 (sc)
ISBN: 978-1-4401-2238-5 (ebook)

Printed in the United States of America

iUniverse rev. date: 03/23/2009

Acknowledgment

The cover image is derived from a photograph taken by Walter Vehrs.

The photograph was of a ship carrying German emigrants leaving Bremerhaven harbor bound for America, much like the ship that carried the Haas family and their hopes and dreams.

The photograph is in the Cuxhaven Archive.

Table of Contents

Introduction

Our father—Vati—was among the thousands who determined to find a better life in America after WW II. As his children, we're glad he did. This book tells his story as only he can—in the first person, as he describes his resolve to emigrate, his reluctant look back at the war that changed everything in his life and his unexpected experiences in becoming a new American.

Kurt Haas was born the middle of five children in Mainz, Germany in 1911. After high school he apprenticed as a custom tailor and at age 23 was the youngest in his class to earn his "Meister-Brief" in 1934. Five years later he was drafted into the German Army where he spent the next six years posted in Germany, Norway, Italy and Austria. As a Christian who believed he had no license to kill others, he was relieved of having to carry a rifle by cleverly insisting that he could not close one eye in order to aim. To this day he thanks God that he escaped the ordeal of the war without firing or receiving a single shot.

This book begins at the war's end and describes how he was determined to make a new life for his family by coming to America. The book ends as he and his family proudly become American citizens in front of Independence Hall in Philadelphia, five years after having stepped off the boat. As we were growing up Vati told us many wonderful stories and we finally insisted that he write them down. Undaunted by the challenge of writing in his non-native tongue, which he did not learn until well into his forties, Vati writes directly and honestly about many of the little and big things that went both wrong and ultimately right for him as he realized his dream come true.

This is Vati's first book. But, as he is a very spry 97 years old now, and because we know of so many more stories that aren't included in this first book, we expect to see a few more from him.

Gerhard Haas
Napa 2009

Why America?

YES, WHY DID I GO TO AMERICA? I had no rich uncle there. I knew nobody in this far away land. Nobody from my folks ever went there. Why did I like to go away from my home country?

In Europe the people say, "Only people without hope of a good future in their own land will do this." Was I at this point in my life? In some ways, yes. Otherwise, why would I go into the unknown world of America? Life after WW II in Germany was very hard, often too hard for me. I was looking for some better way out of my daily unsuccessful routine.

After WW II, most German cities lay in ruins—cities like Bremen and Mainz—the home towns of my wife Gertrud and me. Then, thanks to the never unforgettable help from Canada and the USA, Germany came back to life. But still in a short time I was at the end of my rope. I had to work day and night just for making a plain living. No wonder that

I was looking for something better for my family. But how? Besides the daily work, I was constantly on the go for food or something else in life. Even to rent a better place to live we could never do. (We lived for seven years in one room. All living space was controlled by city fathers and to move into another simple apartment, I would have to pay about four to five thousand Deutsch Marks up front—lost money—on top of the high rent.) Before we had the new Deutsch Marks, we had money, but could buy nothing except on the black market. Then after 1948, we could buy everything, but now we had no money, and the daily struggle for me was still the same. Somehow I started playing with the idea to go to America. I liked the idea to do something better. Why not? Other people did it, why not I? But some came back from their dreamland with bad stories; they didn't like it. Then some friend said to me, "Don't listen to them; they gave up too early. If you really go—and when you go by boat and you are in the middle of the ocean, you have to take off your shoes and your stockings and throw them over board into the water below—then you will never come back!" This I never did. But right on that boat I made up in my mind that I will stay in America and never come back! This was a good decision and I still like to be here.

But, like in all the rest of the world, there is nothing for nothing, so this I write on the following pages. Would I ever do it again? I was already forty-three years old when I left Germany. Next time I would come much earlier in life and maybe then become a millionaire; who knows? But with all that I do have now, I am a happy man. That's all what counts most. The Bible says, "For what does it profit a man to gain the whole world and forfeit his life?"

"Mr. Haas, please tell me why you want to go to America?" It was after W W II and I was sitting in front of the US Consul at Frankfurt/Main. The question gave me a start. I had to answer quickly, but somehow I hesitated with my words. Suddenly there was too much going through my mind all at once. Why – why did the Consul ask this strange almost funny question? Why did I want to go to America? What should I answer? Didn't the Consul himself know why the poor people of Germany wanted to go to America? At this time all of the people of Europe were having a very hard time just making a decent living. The great W W II was just over and for many people the daily life was just a question of survival, nothing more. But, maybe the US Consul was not touched by our way of life. He was an American and at this time in Germany an American was a person out of his normal world. America was a country, or a world full of hope—splendid expectations, fullness of life, with a great and almost unimaginable future. America was to us left over people from W W II like a paradise in our always struggling and miserable existence. But, in this short moment before my answer to the Consul, there was something else going through my mind. I had lived all those years under the well known Nazi regime. I didn't like it, but there was no way out.

I also had two little children at the time, and if at all possible, I wanted to give them a better chance at an education than I had. The only answer for me was, "America."

So I said, "Mr. Consul, I want the freedom of your country, and I also want to have a better living standard for my family, that's all."

The Consul smiled, "Mr. Haas, in our country you may have all you wish for. You will have your freedom of religion or politics or choice of workplace; nobody will ever be in your personal way. There is only one point I want to tell you about right now. Please adjust to our laws and the order of our country, and there will be no limit to your education and freedom. It's in your hands now and I wish you good luck."

But, going to America wasn't as easy as it may appear at this writing. The day I left the office of the Consul had only come at the end of an almost endless paperwork struggle of preparation. Now, after almost two years of hope, I finally had all the necessary papers in my hand and the door was wide open for the new, unknown adventure of immigrating to America. And I would never forget all the events leading up to it.

Two years earlier my mother had asked me the same question the US Consul had asked, "Kurt, why do you want to go to America?" The day I told my mother I wanted to go to America, she just asked me this one question, nothing else; then she fell silent. She looked straight into my eyes, but said nothing. She looked as if she was in a different world, one that I had never seen before, as if she needed time, much time to grasp this totally new and strange announcement from me. Why was going to America such a strange thing to her? I began to feel uneasy also; had I hurt her? What was so wrong to want to go to America and to improve the condition of my family? I was still in my best years and America was a good country. Here in Germany I had nothing to lose and with some effort I could have a better life in the new world, better than what we had in our now poor and devastated Germany.

I remembered the time when my father saw the destruction of the bombing in our hometown and said to mother, "Who in the world will ever rebuild this once great city? All the houses and most of the living quarters are gone. Nobody can ever do it, nobody."

It was true. American bombers and others had ruined the city, but that was war and it was the same all over Europe. Now the war was over and no other country except America helped us so much to get back on our feet. But slowly, too slowly for me and others, were the hard times going away. And I was no man for the black market, living from day to day without a clear vision for a better future. No wonder America was my answer, but mother was still thinking.

I kept on talking. "Mother, you still have two daughters here at home. I will write you often."

Then mother suddenly asked, "Why is it America? Aren't you afraid to live alone in that strange country? You know we have no relatives over there. I think you don't really know what you have in mind to do. Going to America? You know no English, you know nobody. You have a family. Tell me why you really want to go to America. You are still young (I was already 42), you are my youngest son and I know more about America than you think. For sure I've never been in America, it is so far from here and so strange to me and my whole way of life. You will never like it and will never be happy when you are away from our nice Rhine region. There is no second Rhine in all the world and no second people like ours. Why do you want to live with the totally mixed people in America? Please don't go. Please stay here right where you were born and believe me that the times will be better. Just learn to wait and forget the whole funny idea of going to America just for a better life. Do you really think the money hangs on trees over there? Anywhere in all the world they only cook with water—please don't leave me alone for the rest of my short life. You also know how I love the children. Tell me, who in the world gave you this crazy idea to forget your homeland and your kinfolks and begin daydreaming about a better future in America?"

What should I say? Mother was older, and maybe she was right. I too had never been to America, I just listened to other people, and read a lot of newspapers. Somehow I got stuck with this idea that America would be my only chance for a good future. There must be something much better across the ocean. I would just have to go and believe that everything would be all right. Many, many others had done the same thing; nobody even once came back after they were gone. So, why not I?

"Mother, you know I am having a very hard time raising my small family since I came back from the war. I just work, work, work from early in the morning until late at night and there is never anything left over. This is more than just depressing and I want to give the children a better education than I can afford now. They should have a better chance in life than I have now, don't you think? America is a good country and would give us all a better future. I read all this in the newspapers from New York."

A good friend of ours was really the reason for my America idea. She once said to me, "Kurt, I watched your business struggle for some time." (She herself was a successful business woman, running a good vegetarian restaurant in my hometown.) "Kurt, you will not progress much here in the future, and you have those two nice children, why don't you give them a better future, maybe in America? Would you like to go to America? My son lives there too and I go every two years to New York City. He always sends the ticket and I see how others make it." (Her son had a successful pharmacy in New York City.) Why not break off here and start something new before you will be too old to do it. After five years most of the immigrants have a little house and garden for themselves. They love their new way of life."

At her last visit, she had brought me the German New York Stats Zeitung (newspaper) and the New York Herald Tribune. I showed my mother, "See, Mother, see how cheap the people live in America today. One dozen eggs are only forty-five cents, here we pay thirty cents for one egg; there one pound of honey is thirty-one cents, here it is 4.5 DM, and there . . ."

"Stop!" said Mother. "Who gives you today a dozen eggs for forty-five cents? This is all big baloney. I don't believe one word of your U.S. newspapers. This is all plain advertisement or propaganda. You should know you can write anything you want in a paper and this paper from America is no exception. Why do you want to so easily believe this strange paper and not your own mother? I know what kind of people are living in America. Don't you think we had enough propaganda all these past years? I know what America is all about."

Then I laughed. "Mother, you've never been in America, how do you know about that country? You've never seen one American, have you? And we don't even have relatives in

America, so how can you know what America is all about?" But Mother kept on talking as if I had said nothing.

"Let me tell you, I know. Leave the Americans alone, let them live their own life. Maybe they are happy too and some of them must be good, but many, many are not good people over there. I know."

This was just too much for me and I asked, "Mother, how in the world can you say that? Have you ever talked to even one American? You haven't."

"Oh, yes, I saw not only one American, I saw two and I will never forget the event. It was a long time ago. I was still in my teens and it happened right in our small home village. You know at that time there wasn't much going on in the lonely countryside, but once in awhile we had some interesting Saturday night specials. For two weeks a placard hung at the village's only inn. 'Two great Americans will come with a very important show doing some educational tricks and performing some new sights, things you have never heard about.' And for sure, at the appointed time the room was packed like a sardine can.

"Everybody went to see and hear these two strangers from across the ocean. At the entrance, one man took the twenty-five cent entrance fee. When everyone had paid and was in the room, the other fellow came out on the small stage. What amazed almost everyone was that they were both black men.

We always thought real Americans were red like Indians, or at least white like we are, but black; who knew of black Americans? But this made the show even more interesting. The next surprise was that the fellow spoke good German and we were wondering how in the world could a black American speak such good German? So, he must be a very educated man from across the ocean.

"And then it came, the wisdom we had never heard of, from far off America. He first addressed the ladies in the room. 'Ladies, you are the most important person in your homes. You are much more important than your men. You have the whole house in order before he comes home and every day you keep it in good shape. And then you ladies always have to do a lot of sewing; you have to do it right, right from the beginning. In doing this you have to be very careful to make a good knot at the end of the thread, otherwise the thread will certainly slip out of the fabric.' But this we all knew long before this fellow with his so-called wisdom came into our village.

"He then had much more of such silly stuff, and started with the men. 'You men are mostly farmers here and you are very important too. But much more important on your farm is your horse. Feed your horse very good in the morning, otherwise it might surely collapse at evening, then in a short time you will go broke. You will remember the story of the farmer who fed his horse less and less until it lay dead in the barn.' (That we knew a long time before this fellow came into our village.) Then he had a lot more silly stuff to say and we wanted to get rid of him so we made a lot of noise. He then said, 'Be patient, until now it's just been jokes but the best part will come soon. We'll have a short intermission, then my friend will have more ideas and surprises for you.' He disappeared behind the curtain and everyone calmed down waiting for the new surprises to come. They came very shortly. A young boy came running into the room shouting, 'They just drove off with their horse and buggy and with the money box and they're gone!' Naturally, the men went wild but in the darkness they couldn't do much. We just laughed and laughed, but some of the men said, 'Now they are going to another village telling them the same junk stuff! But for now, no more Americans in our village; no more American wisdom.'"

Then Mother asked, "Don't you know what the Bible says? 'Thou shalt dwell in the land of your fathers and thus shall you be fed.'

"There was in the village a savings and loan bank. One day an inspector from the city came and looked into the books of the clerk. In the morning we were in the field and the clerk was seen going very quickly into the nearby forest. Later that evening it was learned that the clerk had disappeared with all the money. Later he wrote a letter from Hamburg. He felt sorry, but when he got to America he would pay everything back. We never heard another word from him.

"Then there was the funny boy living with a farmer. He never worked when he was needed, he just hung around the tap rooms. He was good for nothing in the village. So the relatives got some money together and sent him to Hamburg in order to go to America. But when he arrived in Hamburg, he sent a letter back, he needed more money for the boat ticket. He promised to pay everything back when he had a good job in America. But nothing came. See, that's the kind of people the stock of America is made of." That was the end of Mother's talk about America. But for myself, I kept studying the New York newspaper, looking for a sponsor or a good connection in order to go overseas.

At this time emigrating from Germany to America was quite an experience. First, I would need a sponsor who was a good citizen of the United States and could guarantee that I would be trouble-free for five years after arriving in the U.S. Then, besides my normal visa, I needed a quota number which took about 18 months to obtain (if you ever appear on the list). I still remember the very first letter I wrote inquiring about life in the U.S. and whether I would be able to make a living there with my family. It was a letter to a man unknown to me, but known to my mother-in-law. Surprisingly, in a short time I received an answer, "Come to America, I will sponsor you and your family. Don't wait any longer. This is a good country. In Europe you just live to work. Here in America you work for a good living. I have a little shop and when I am retired soon, I will give it to you. Get your papers ready and come."

What an offer! No wonder I wanted to go to America. This was just the opportunity I was waiting for. Now the door was open for all of my emigration dreams. It was still true, everyone needs a little luck and this was mine, so I took it. The only problem was the quota number from the U.S. consulate in Frankfurt. I waited and waited for fourteen months, but there was no answer; how could I get to New York? Then a letter came from my sponsor, "Why didn't you come? I have retired and had to sell my shop. I couldn't wait any longer for you to come. I now live in upstate New York. When you do come, you will have to help yourself, but I will still sponsor you anyway." This was strange news coming from my dreamland across the ocean—"help yourself?" How could I do this in a strange land?

My wife said, "We have no relatives or friends in the United States, what do you think will happen? We can't sit on our luggage at the harbor in New York. We don't know English, how can we help ourselves? Don't you think we really have to forget the whole nicely planned expedition to your wonderland over the ocean?"

There it was. After almost fourteen months of waiting and waiting to go—nothing. I said, "Let's wait one more week and if nothing special happens, then we will really forget the whole plan, and Mother will surely be very happy to hear this decision."

When Mother heard about the bad news from America, she just laughed, "I told you, didn't I tell you before what kind of people are living in America? There is just too much baloney and swindling in this far-away country across the ocean. It's no wonder, and this is just the beginning. What will it be like when you are really on your own and start living over there?

"You should know it's always the same story. The kids are like their fathers or even worse, I know." Mother kept on, "Didn't I tell you before from my experience in my home village? Those poor people didn't know any better, but you should learn from this and I think you should at least listen to your mother and your wife. Forget the whole idea of going to America with your family."

After three days of waiting, a letter arrived from Philadelphia, USA, a letter from my Wonderland. I didn't know the sender, whose name was Jakob Wasenmiller, Minister. With the letter in hand, I ran to my wife, "Gertrud, I think we now have made it. An American Minister is writing to us about our emigrating, can you imagine? A Minister writing to me?" (A Minister in Germany is like a Secretary of State.)

But Gertrud said, "Hold on, first we have to look in the dictionary to see what the word means." We both looked and I calmed down. A minister in America is only a preacher or pastor. Nevertheless, the letter was well written. Somehow this pastor from Philadelphia had gotten my name from my sponsor in New York who couldn't help me and now this new man would take over our emigration process. He and his wife invited us to come to Philadelphia since he was looking for new German immigrants and would pick us up at the harbor in New York. We should not worry about anything, and he wrote that he would help us to get started in the new world of America. If necessary, he would even help us with money for the trip to New York.

My, things suddenly couldn't be better for me and my planned trip across the ocean. Now I began to organize ideas in my head for the trip. I must pay the ship fares for four people. I must sell everything I owned, which fortunately (or unfortunately) wasn't much. I must make more trips to the U.S. Consulate to renew my quota number, and many more such things. And now, even my Mother, after also reading the letter from the minister, wanted to help me as she saw my determination to go. Even other relatives gave me financial support. My sister bought our piano, even though she couldn't play it, and others also got excited about our plans.

An old friend gave me a huge steamer trunk, and while I was transporting it, another friend, Emil, met me on the street near the Rhine riverbank promenade. "Hey Kurt, what's going on? Are you taking a big trip?"

"Oh, yes, what's so strange about that?" I replied.

"With this great trunk? In the old times people used this monstrosity to go to America. What place are you going to?" he asked.

"America!" When he heard this, he was shocked.

"America? You? You're going to America? You must be crazy! What in the world will you do in America? Have you ever been there? Have you a rich uncle there?"

"No, it will be the first time I've ever crossed the ocean, but I want to stay there forever."

Emil looked at me as if from a very long distance and then slowly said, "Do you see the Rhine River in front of us? Kurt, Kurt, come to your senses, you're just making a joke aren't you? In all honesty, how do you have the guts to leave here? In your America there is nothing like the Rhine River, and there is no city like our Mainz. Don't you realize why Americans so often come here and take a Rhine River trip on the fine white boats? It is always the high point of their lifetime. This is almost the nicest spot on earth, otherwise they would never come in busloads from all over the world. Kurt, before you make the biggest mistake of your life, think it over. I could never do this—go away from here—never!"

I answered, "Emil, my mother always said 'What good is the dinner table if you only enjoy beautiful but empty plates?' Sometime later I too will take a nice Rhine River trip like the rich Americans do, you will see. This is the first step in my new experience. Do you remember when we were kids and handled the huge suitcases for the rich American boat travelers into the fine hotels? They always gave us a few pennies, but we always thought we wanted to be Americans too, traveling around the world with big suitcases and pockets full of dollars."

We both laughed and Emil said, "Kurt, you are right, we always wanted to be rich Americans in those days, but to go now? To really break up everything here and to actually go over there, that's a very different story. Anyhow, Kurt, if you really want to do this, I wish you good luck even though I feel sorry for you. Even if I had to die I would never go from here. I want to be buried with my folks right here near the Rhine."

During the preparations for the trip, there were always other people who wanted to give me advice about my new American adventure. Sometimes I wondered what if there really was some truth in all their talk. Like the famous Don Quixote, could I really be making a big mistake taking my family to an unknown continent? Then my life might be worse than it was before and there would be no going back to

Germany. I would have no money for a return trip and there would be no money to rent an apartment to live in.

After much thought, I decided to ask an old friend of my father who sometimes visited his children in California. If he should talk negatively like all the other people I would not make the mistake of going to America, leaving my hometown and losing everything. I would stay right here, no matter what.

When I talked to this man about the trip and my desire to make a better living in America he said without hesitation, "Why not? If you are determined to go you should go. America is a great and good land and you will make it. It is a country for ambitious people and there is always an opportunity for the right one. You will make it, you have a good profession and America is a free country.

"Nobody, but nobody will ever bother you about your private life. The only thing I fear is that your children will have it too good. Most Americans cannot raise children the right way; they spoil them too much because they cannot forget the hard life they themselves had when they came into the land. They want their children to have a better life, but in many cases it doesn't work out for the good. The trouble is that you won't know this until it is too late and you better be watching out right in the beginning.

"Another point is that many immigrants want to convert the Americans to their old German way of thinking. You know, your hometown is almost two thousand years old and you grew up here with this great history and you will miss this heritage. America is only a few hundred years old, there is not much to talk about for us, but they also have something which makes them proud of their country. When I visited my folks over there we strolled through the historic houses like my grandmother had, full of antique junk; cowboy cabins and rotten horse barns, full of old time stuff; old Indian clothing, dusty buggies and old fashioned tools. But that is their history, different from what we have here. Their life began not so long ago and many of their forefathers came from Germany helping to shape the way of life in this new country. Don't expect too much from a young country, but respect their heritage too. Theirs is a great blessing in doing so, even if it is different from our life, don't you think?"

This was a good talk and I went home that night saying to myself, I'm going no matter what. What other people can do, I can do also. I know, I will burn a bridge behind me. My parents from both sides came from old German farmland and for almost ten generations my relatives lived around the same village area in Eastern Germany. It was all gone for them too. How many bridges did we burn after WW II? We lost everything through bombing and burning. When this great war was over there was nothing left for me and my wife, everything we had before went up in fire and smoke. My wife

19

rescued only one small suitcase with some clothing of mine and when we started our life again it was very strenuous for all of us.

The same week that my sponsor from New York had canceled his support for me in America I had also received a letter from the US Consulate about my long awaited quota number: we could go in about four weeks. What should I do? I had no place in New York or in the USA to go to, and so I had postponed my hearing (they put me right under the pile of the other papers). But now with the letter from the minister from Philadelphia the situation was quite different. Now I had positive hope and again went to the U.S. Consul at Frankfurt. I wanted to renew my application for the quota number, but when I got to the Consulate office, every building was closed. What was going on? It was midweek, and not a holiday. Why was nothing open? I asked the guard at the entrance about it and he said it was a great American holiday and every business would be closed until Monday. "What great American holiday?" I asked.

"They are celebrating the Fourth of July, but what do you want to do at the Consulate?" the guard asked.

"Get my papers ready to go to America," I answered.

"You want to go to America forever, and you don't know what the Fourth of July means to them? You better hurry and learn English and American history or they'll ship you right back when you arrive in New York," he warned.

I didn't have much time to learn English now, but my sister, who had learned English in school said, "Kurt, English is very easy. They have a simple grammar and once you are over there you will catch on fast. You know the English stole their language the same way they stole their empire. When they came around the oceans and found a lonely island they raised the Union Jack and said, 'Now you are English, now you belong to us.' They did the same with their language. In English you find words from all over Europe. They mixed all those languages together in a huge pot and out came English."

So I had to go again the next week and the clerk said, "We put you right under the hearing papers. You'll have to wait and we will let you know." After four weeks I went to the office again, but the answer was the same, "We will let you know, maybe in three months you will go."

But a clerk nearby said, "You come back next week again. There is always somebody who cannot go and then we will put you on the top of the list." This is what I did and the clerk said, "You are lucky, come again next week and bring all of your papers with you, this time we mean business."

"What kind of papers?" I asked.

"First you have to bring an official record stating whether or not you were ever a Nazi or a member of any SS organization. Then you have to bring the complete record of your life from the police department of your town, for you as well as your family. Then you have to bring the entire record of your medical history, including all immunizations and other family information."

"Is that all?" I asked.

"For the moment, yes," he answered.

At the police department I had to get records of all financial business involving the city and county, such as all tax records. With all of the other requirements, I was on the run the whole week getting everything together, but I was back in Frankfurt at the Consul's office the next week. The clerk instructed me, "Now you have to return with your whole family to our medical department for personal health inspections and X-rays." So in a few days, all four of our little family went to Frankfurt again to see the doctors. When all the examinations and X-rays were done I said to the doctor, "Doctor, you must have the best people living in your America?"

He laughed, "Yes, we have. We are a very special people and we want to take only the best from the German crowd." To my surprise, we passed all the tests and the clerk promised me the completed papers in about four weeks. In the meantime, I needed to look for a ship to travel on. Now I was really getting excited! I could really go into the new world. Now things started going too fast for me. America wasn't so far away anymore. It was unbelievable, but it was becoming true.

At home, I had to put everything in order and start selling everything we wouldn't need in America in order to pay our fare on the ship and then clean our apartment. The week before leaving town by train, I had to go to the police department to report my leaving, as was the custom in Germany (and still is today). While at the office the policeman asked, "Haas, why do you want to go to America? Is our country not good enough for you anymore? You were born here. Do you think that over there the money will hang on trees?" This man resembled my father, who had died about twelve years before. The policeman's words put a lump in my throat, and it was the first time I really fully felt what I was doing. Then he continued in a friendly tone, "Haas, anyhow, I wish you good luck. Write a letter to us when you have it good. Maybe you will be the lucky ones." When he shook hands with me I almost wanted to cry and a strange feeling came over me, but it was now too late to think about not going. I had to go now no matter what. And somehow I knew it would really be better for me and our family.

Coming back to our apartment, everything looked so empty after the last of the furniture buyers had picked up everything. It frightened me, now that I had nothing left of my own to see. Then I looked around for the last of my most precious belongings, the papers. Where were they? I looked around and could find them nowhere in the empty rooms. I asked Gertrud, "Do you have any of our papers? Do you have the big brown envelope with the documents?"

"No, the last person who was in the room cleaned everything and put all the trash in the waste basket down in the cellar," Gertrud explained. "Early tomorrow morning the lady who lives above us will make a fire under the wash kettle and burn all of the waste paper."

I listened in shock. Our precious papers; all the documents, the passports, the ship tickets, the visas and the money; the billets for the trip to Bremerhaven and all the other important statements were all in this one envelope and it could all be lost in the fire under the kettle. It would be the worst thing that could possibly happen. I would be the poorest man in town. Gertrud and I raced down the stairway into the basement and spread all the waste paper around looking for my brown envelope. At the very bottom of the box I fished the brown envelope out of the trash. Oh, thank God! Were we ever happy! The lady from upstairs came in and asked, "What in the world are you doing here with all this mess? You must be crazy. What do you want with trash in America, pulling everything apart like you are searching for gold?" When I explained to her what had happened she cried, "Holy Maria!

What would you have done if I had burned all of your papers tomorrow morning?"

I said, "It would have been: Goodbye America, I would have to go to the welfare department."

Happily our plans didn't end in tragedy. I was very happy with all of our papers in hand and the next day we left for Bremerhaven, our first step in getting to America by ship, and the port where all emigrants say their last farewells to their former fatherland.

Bremerhaven

Our last station in Germany before leaving for America was the Great Emigration House in Bremerhaven. Now I would be one of the thousands of people who would leave from here to go to America starting as early as 1847, when the first of the American steamboats started taking people across the Atlantic. People from all parts of Europe had sailed across the ocean from this place. On some days there were as many as 6,000 people leaving from these rooms by the sea, with everyone full of hope for a better living in America. I had read old reports describing how the emigrants had left, many with barely the clothes on their backs; no money, no relatives, their only hope that life would be better there. For many, it was the last grasp at the straw of life.

Now I was one of them too, but in comparison to many before me I was rich. My trip was paid for and I had $100 in my pocket which my mother had given me. I was still in my best years and all four of us were healthy and trusted in

God at all times. What more did we need? What a modern adventure it was in our daily life, all just to have a better way of living. I knew it was a risky adventure, but I had also learned that without risking something, you gain nothing.

I kept arranging all of our suitcases (except for the big monster box that was already on the ship) while waiting to board, on what seemed like the endless Columbus Quay. Beside and around me, filling the whole vast area lining the open water were people, nothing but people, people and more people. All kinds of emigrants like me; relatives, friends, well wishers, former club members with great banners, singing groups and brass bands, all talking and shouting. The restless noisy throng waiting to board the ship seemed like a vast colony of constantly moving ants.

When my little son Gerhard saw the only ship at the quay he was astonished. "Daddy -what? - with this little thing of a ship are we going to America? That's impossible." From our talks before he always had the impression that we were going on a really large super ocean liner to the New World, and now there was only this small ship in which to cross the ocean, bobbing along the great pier.

But there was absolutely no other boat around, so I said, "That's it, do you see a bigger boat? We will make it, otherwise they would not take us today for the trip."

Suddenly a voice came over the loudspeakers to the waiting crowd, "All aboard, this will be the last ship of the season. If you miss it there will be no more ocean crossings this year."

Now that was the signal of the year. Eagerly everyone walked up the gangplank, almost as long ago, when old Noah went with all his animals into the Ark. Pair by pair with all of our heavy luggage we all disappeared into the boat, looking for our cabins. Then we soon returned on deck, crowding the steering side toward the waiving noisy people left down on the pier. What a farewell! We really were leaving Germany! What a sensation. Would we ever see any of our good folks again?

At the railing beside me stood a tall man who was absorbing all of the impressions and unusual sights around us. He was really moved by this farewell party for so many people on the endless quay. Then he said to me, "This is fantastic! This picture you will see only once in the whole world. I always love it. Look, the people down there almost leap into the water beside the boat. What excitement! What emotion here and there, just for leaving friends and relatives, for going to America, maybe never to return again." He kept on talking, "I travel a lot around the world, but a farewell party of emigrants as in Bremerhaven, that you have to see. This goes to your heart; it's so thrilling to me. Are you an emigrant too?" He kept on telling me about his trips around the world as an evangelist and now he was going home to Seattle in the U.S., having been a missionary in Europe. I could tell he was excited.

Suddenly the boat came to life. It shuddered all over, then slowly but steadily, the distance to the quay became wider. We really were moving away from the land, leaving everyone behind. It was almost heartbreaking. The people cried, laughed, waved and shouted. On the pier the brass band played old German folk songs which made some of the people homesick right there at the beginning of their journey. No wonder! It was so sensational here in Bremerhaven. Down on the quay stood a crowd of over 1,500 people, making enough noise for those on board as if they were giving their life away. Some yelled, "If you don't like it over there, come back! You don't have to stay there forever. Write a letter soon. Did you hear me?"

A middle aged lady beside me shouted down, "Oh greet my mother—mother. Oh, I'll see you no more. Mother, what am I doing?" She cried and cried and waved her wet handkerchief until the excitement became less and less and the pier became smaller and smaller. For many it now became a quiet sobering moment; a personal historical event, the very beginning of the new life in the hoped for better country.

The children had their fun and excitement with all of the new things and sights, but my wife and I stood and looked and looked over the whirling waters below, back toward our dwindling homeland which gradually disappeared in a gray fog until we were all alone on the great quiet sea. Standing at the back of the boat we were hoping for the best to come and fighting tears and emotions resulting from taking this great step of our life into the unknown. Was it really all true?

Darkness came on fast. The long day was gone and also gone was the excitement of leaving our homeland and gone was the connection to our former world with all the ways of living we had known. And just now, all these things dissolved before our eyes into the dark water below, leaving me alone with only the thoughts of going to America and sailing into my "better dreamland."

In my life I had dreamed many dreams, and now some of them were being fulfilled. Why should it be so different and at the same time so impossible to experience?

Our first big surprise came as we descended the stairways to our assigned rooms. We looked for real cabins with berths as you would expect on ocean liners, or even on a small ship like this one. But for this long trip to New York, there were no cabins or berths, just plain steel bunk beds, with separate quarters for men and women. We were on the lowest passenger deck, right at the water line. Even as a family we would not be together all of the time. When I saw the sea water slapping on the round porthole at my bedside I just hoped there would be no leaks or opening for water to spill into the rooms. It reminded me of my time as a soldier when

I went on the troop transport ships to Norway in WW II. On that trip we also had to sleep down by the water line with fifty men in a small room. But today, it would be better than back then. Today there was no fear of getting hit by English submarines or bombs from airplanes falling out of the sky. The time was totally different now, and in about eleven days this public living would be all over, and we would start real life again.

Another surprise was the discovery of the first sign of the new American culture, the wire coat hanger. Never in my life had I seen a wire hanger and we all laughed at this funny thing in our hands. Was this the beginning of the new time of luxury we were approaching? I had a heavy overcoat and when I hung it on the wire, it just fell to the floor; I would need three wire hangers to hold it. But in the end, it turned out to be a very practical thing for the need of the moment. But I had never thought that this would turn out to be the way clothing was hung all the time in America. (I later learned of the many other good uses for a wire coat hanger. With this hanger you could open a car door if locked out, you could clean a plugged toilet or even make a flower arrangements and all manner of other crafts.) Soon we had everything in order, and the bell rang for evening dinner.

We rushed up on deck where three other stairways opened into the huge dining room. All the people, mostly all emigrants like us filled the place fast, expecting good food from the serving waiters. (First class passengers dined separately.) Everybody was glad to be in a nice place like this, we even had printed menu cards at the tables and we all studied the details of the coming meal. My, this will be our first American dinner, what will it be? Then we read the printed dinner card:

Dinner	
Soups	Cream of Asparagus, Custard Consume
Fish	Boiled Southampton Turbot, Sauce Hollandaise, Parsley
Main Dishes	Roast Philadelphia Chicken, Gravy
Potatoes	Boiled, Mashed, French Fried
Vegetables	Fresh Carrots, Succotash, Cauliflower Polonaise
Salads	Lettuce, Beet Root, Spanish Frisco
Dressing	Thousand Island, Catsup
Desserts	Prince Puechler Ice Cream, Macaroons, Assorted Cheese, Fruit
Beverages	Coffee, Tea, Chamomile, Peppermint
10 P.M.	Assorted Sandwiches

Gerhard said, "What is it? This must be the new American food. We'll just have to learn better English or we won't know what we are eating." Then the waiters came with the food and after it was served we all laughed. It was just plain good old German food which we knew well from the homeland. Nothing special, but we all liked it and did enjoy this first meal on the boat. When we were filled we went down to our bunk beds, very tired, and slept like never before after our first day of adventure on the high seas on the way to America.

But I didn't sleep so well. My mind was still full of all the impressions of the past few days, in contrast to the overbearing bureaucracy and poor living conditions after WW II. We had lived for seven years in one room and there was no way to improve our condition. Almost every room in Germany was under the control of the city fathers and not even with money could one improve the situation. On the same floor, besides my family in our one room, had lived my mother-in-law, sister-in-law, grandmother and the landlord. We all used the same toilet and the same kitchen. We just had to stick together. In the same room my first daughter was born and died after living only two days. She had just stopped breathing, and in those poor times, even the doctor could not help. For this little one there was no funeral service. The carpenter made a little coffin and I put Ursula in it and with the box under my arm, went to the cemetery beside our house. The grave digger made a hole at the end of the place, I put her in and we closed the little grave.

But now, with the constant vibration of the boat, I felt that all this was being shaken from my shoulders. It was all behind me now; the ocean separated me from past events and now I was a free man. I felt greatly relieved from the overwhelming stress and tomorrow—tomorrow I would have something to look forward to. I finally fell asleep with these thoughts.

The next day everyone was strolling around the deck, talking with fellow emigrants or just sitting in one of those lounge chairs, doing nothing. I did the same—what a super relaxed feeling. Now I was on the last boat of the year going with so many other emigrants to America, looking far out into the ever moving sea and enjoying a great sense of relaxation. Also on this ship my inner unrest and troubled emotions from all of the business of arranging the departure disappeared right into the ocean and the surrounding atmosphere. I felt I was becoming a new person. This trip was paid for and now for about twelve days my little family had enough to eat; we had a place to sleep and then we would all be in America. This dissolved all of the remaining anxiety. I thought, why not? Others did it, so will I—my, what self-confidence for a poor little fellow like me

"Hi, Mr. Immigrant, what are you dreaming about?" The missionary from Seattle stood beside me and then also sat down on one of the lounge chairs. "Let's talk a little." We exchanged names.

"You are right, Mr. Wagner, the weather is so nice here and today I feel great on this ship," I responded. "Was I dreaming? Yes, sometimes dreams don't come true, but now, my daydream of going to America is coming true right now. I feel great. All my former tension is gone. All the former wartime and post-wartime impressions are disappearing right into the water below."

"Yes, I think you emigrants must be happy to get away from so troubled a country and go to America. Say, Mr. Haas," he asked, "why are you going to America?"

"Oh, Mr. Wagner, you are asking the same question as the US Consul in Frankfurt," I replied.

"I know what you mean, but do you have a rich uncle in America, or someone who will help you over there?" he asked.

"I have nobody over there, only some unknown minister of my church who will pick us up at New York harbor," I explained.

"You know a minister? Then you must be a Christian," he asked.

"I am, otherwise I would not make this trip into the unknown."

"Then you must have some good experience with your God?" he half asked.

"I have," I went on. "I have had many. My whole life is one great experience with the help of God. How could I forget?"

"Oh, were you in the war too?" he asked.

"Oh yes," I explained, "for the whole time. And you know, I came out with nothing left, but with many good experiences."

"You have to tell me about them," he said. "We will be together here for almost twelve days and we have nothing to do all day long. Is it not a great time to talk together about how great our God is all the time? What was your best experience?"

"You know, many people think war is always a horrible event, and it is in some great way. The best war is never any good and always comes out different than planned. You want to hear about my best experience of the war? I don't know if you will believe what I will tell you, but it is true, absolutely true. Do you remember May 8, 1945?"

"Oh yes, the war ended in Europe,'" he said.

"On this day I came from death to life—an angel helped me," I began.

"May 8th was the first day of peace or the last day of the war—who will ever know? But on the night before, I marched with my regiment down from the area near the Alps, into the Danube Valley of Austria. It was a beautiful day and we figured we would be at the U.S. line late on the afternoon of May 8th. We were between the Russian and the U.S. lines and the best thing would be to get into the U.S. camp. But the Russians had different plans. They sent airplanes and bombed our marching columns. After that came the huge tanks and because we couldn't run away, we now were thinking that we would almost certainly become Russian POWs. We had needed to march only another five kilometers and the war would have a good ending for us, but now it would be all over. After five and a half years as a soldier and nine months of marriage I was suddenly standing right in front of a huge Russian tank. It was terrible! The Russian soldiers shook their balled fists at us and shouted, 'Heil Moscow! Berlin Kaput! Hitler Kaput, Heil Moscow!' I though my end would be in Siberia and there seemed no way out.

"I didn't want to go to Siberia and I prayed right by the tank, 'Dear God, please let me go home and not to Siberia.' Then the Russians turned us around in the road and we started marching back along the same road we had been on since that morning. This was to be the end of thousands of German soldiers and the date was May 8, 1945.

"I could not believe this, would there be no way out? We kept marching until suddenly we were ordered to halt. Across the street was a German POW camp with Russian POWs in it. Many Slavic people worked on nearby farms. Now the Russian soldiers opened the gates wide and the poor fellows streamed out and over to us.

"We still had some good things like clothing and other items and the POWs could use everything and anything we had. I found my way around the tumult and peered over the old wooden camp fence. I thought, tonight we will all be in this camp and once I'm behind barbed wires there will be no escape for me. That will be the end.

"At that moment, I felt a firm touch on my right shoulder and a voice saying, 'You have to flee.' I turned around to see who was speaking but there was no one. I thought, maybe you are nervous; this must just be my imagination. But again, the firm voice spoke, 'You have to flee right away, there is not much time.' Now my mind raced. How could I flee from here? Those Russians will shoot at me or jump at me when I'm running away. But the voice was again urging me 'You have to flee and you must leave everything right here.' I only had a small shoulder bag with some letters from home, pictures, my pocket Bible and my Agfa camera, plus some other small articles that I would like to use even in a Russian camp. But again the voice urged, 'Your time is up, you have to go, it is your last chance to get away from the Russians. Hurry,

hurry.' I had to make the decision very quickly, so I threw my shoulder bag on the wagon, slipped around the horses and just faded away.

"There was a frontage road and slowly putting my cap under my arm, as if I were just strolling, I started down that road. I would never want to be in this condition again; my back was cold as ice, my front was hot like an oven. I thought my heart would jump right out of my throat, it was pumping so wildly. I didn't look back and nobody shot at me or ran after me. I kept on walking and walking until I saw a small farmhouse in the distance. I just fell into the door, totally exhausted. Down the road a tank rumbled by without seeing me."

"Oh, Mr. Haas, what a story," my friend said. "An angel must have given you advice about how to get away from the Russian army. How did it feel to be free?"

"Free? Mr. Wagner, I was only half free. The farmer in the house asked, 'Did you run away from the Russians? It won't help you very much.' I pleaded, 'Please show me the fastest way to the Americans; they must be in the nearest village.' The farmer advised me, 'You're wrong. The Americans are about 35 kilometers away from here, didn't you hear it on the radio? This morning they announced that all of the territory south of the River Enns now belongs to the Russian Army, and everything north of the river belongs to the U.S. Army. At midnight the Russians will close all bridges to the German soldiers, so why don't you stay here? I can't run away either and I don't think the Russians are so bad; they'll let you go home in a short while, you will see.'

"'Mr. Farmer,' I replied, 'now I'm only half free. I have to be really free and that will be in the U.S. camp.'

"'You crazy Germans, you want everything right away, how will you walk the distance in unknown territory? They will catch you again any minute.' Suddenly he changed his mind, 'See,' he said, 'go through my garden in the back, you will have to cross a river and then go through the forest to Steyr, that's the place where the old stone bridge is. You have to be across the stone bridge by midnight! Good luck!'

"I went in the way he'd showed, but at the river there was no bridge to cross. I didn't want to swim and get my clothing wet so late in the day. I went around an old barn to look for a little boat, when suddenly I ran into a bunch of farm workers. When they saw me, they talked wildly in a Slavic language. I thought they must be Russian or Polish workers, as we Germans had used them during the war. Now I was in a mess. What will they do with me? I couldn't run away and they could easily kill me. We looked at each other for a moment, then a tall fellow, maybe the foreman, came over and asked me, 'What do you want here?'

"'Do you have a little boat to cross the river?' I asked. 'We have no boat; you wait,' he said and ran back behind the barn. The others kept watching me and I didn't know what to do. Then the man came back with a black bundle under his arm. 'Here, mach schnell,' he ordered. 'You change your uniform for my coat, mach schnell!' When I changed my army uniform coat for his black coat, the whole gang laughed and laughed. The coat was much too big for me and I must have looked very funny. Then he said again, 'Mach schnell, the bridge is only three kilometers down the river—go, go!'

"I took his advice and hurried away. Now I looked almost civilian, with my big black coat, and the tanks didn't suspect anything as they rolled down the road. What a good fellow I thought. Later I found the bridge and went into the forest, but where was Steyr? About an hour later at sundown, I met a heavy German army truck. He was driving the other direction right into Russian hands. I flagged him down and told him we must be in Steyr at midnight. He let me climb on and changed his course and we raced over the highway toward Steyr.

"As darkness came the roads began to overflow with all kinds of fleeing soldiers running toward Steyr into U.S. territory. It got so crowded that vehicles couldn't drive on the road, and the whole army of ours seemed to spread and disappear right into the Austrian forest. We walked and walked until somebody shouted. 'There is Steyr—here are the Americans!' The weary men dropped by the thousands to sleep right at the river bank. But a very small group kept walking; we wanted to see the Americans first and then rest. After a very long hike, I met the first U.S. soldier in WW II who asked us all kinds of military questions. Behind the group of U.S. soldiers I saw the old stone bridge over the river. My happiness was unbounded! That must be the bridge to freedom! The soldiers let us go across the bridge into the U.S. camp. Just at the bridge I looked at my pocket watch, it was 11:30 PM, just time enough to cross. Once on the other side I wanted to shout into the air, 'Oh God, I thank you for sending the angel to get me here in time, by myself I would never have made it!' I gladly walked into the American hands.

"The next morning I learned that the Russian tanks had come at 12:00 midnight and closed the bridge. Nobody could go into the U.S .camp. All the fellows who thought they were in the U.S. camp became Russian POWs. Later they were shipped in boxcars to Russia and many came home sick or not at all. It taught me a lesson, half free is nothing, you have to be one hundred percent free." This ended my first story for Mr. Wagner on board the Neptunia on the way across to America.

The ship's bell was ringing again and we went to lunch. After lunch we had a very leisurely time learning to play bingo and shuffleboard on the deck. Then suddenly far out on the sea there appeared something mildly green above the water. What was it? A sailor standing nearby told me, "This green picture? Today we are very lucky, there is no fog and this green you see is just plain old Ireland, the evergreen island near England." It did look fantastic, like a real mirage coming right out of the ocean.

The captain gave us an inside ship tour and showed us some of the usually unseen machinery in the engine room. The day went quickly; dinner time came, and afterwards we saw a comic movie followed by a late night snack. Tired and full of impressions we went down to our bunk beds on "C" Deck: men to the left, women to the right. We got used to it.

The next morning Mr. Wagner was already on deck in his lounge chair waiting for me. "Hi, good morning Mr. Wagner. How was the sleeping last night after my long story?" I asked.

"Yes, your story must be a great experience for you, a real angel gave you advice on how to get away from the Russians, otherwise I think it would be horrible to be in a POW camp, always behind barbed wire. But didn't you tell me before that there is another side of the war? What did you mean by that?"

"Mr. Wagner, I will tell you some of my own experiences on the other side that not many people know about, but it happens in every war around the world, only in different ways." We were sitting on the deck as we had the day before, looking out at the ocean. We had plenty of time so I went back in my mind to the year 1940 in Northern Germany.

"See, Mr. Wagner, I told you yesterday how afraid I was to go into the POW camp in Austria because I knew what POW camps were all about. I was there in the first years of the war for almost nine months. Should I tell you this story too?"

"Please, I would like to hear it," Mr. Wagner replied. "I don't often have the opportunity to listen to a person who was involved in things like that."

"I guess you know how quickly France collapsed in 1940, after which thousands of French POWs came into Germany," I began. "The division I was in should have gone to fight in France, but with France, the war was over so quick, we all received new orders. So I was transferred into a brand new POW camp in Northern Germany to work as foreman of the clothing department there. Our camp was a repair place for many other POWs with about 500 men in it. I had about ninety POWs in my workroom. Others worked in shoe repair rooms and others did other kinds of camp work. I slept outside the camp, but early every morning I went in and at 6:00 PM I went out.

"You see, life in a POW camp is naturally very different from a so-called normal life. It is a life-style itself, always full of hope for something better, but nothing better comes all day long. All too soon the daily course ends up in a boring routine. There is no way out, the whole world ends up at the huge borders inside the barbed wire fence around the four corners of the camp. For intelligent young men it is a very small world and there's no room for ambitious people.

"Very often I felt the same way. In the morning the camp guard let me in through the barbed wire fence door and closed the heavy wooden door after me. I was locked in for the whole day. Many times I had the feeling that I was a prisoner of this war machinery myself, but for how long? I didn't know. Nobody knew. We just had to wait.

"My interpreter was a man from Paris named Jacque. He was a very intelligent helper, a real Frenchman, and the two of us ran the workroom together. Before long the people discovered I had a camera. Picture taking was my hobby, even in wartime. Jacque came to me with a request. 'Mr. Haas, will you do us a favor? Some of our men have the idea to send pictures home to their girlfriends for Christmas. Will you do this and take pictures of our men here to send back home? You also for sure must have a girl at home, don't you?' What a question. In wartime to send pictures back home from a POW camp? I could not do this on my own authority. I went to the camp guard officer and he was agreeable, saying, 'Why not? Give the fellows some happiness in this miserable life, but take pictures only of the men themselves and bring them to us. We will put a stamp on the back side, and everything will be OK.'

"This was good news for the men at the camp, so one sunny day I lined them up one by one against the wall of our barracks and shot them very precisely with my Agfa camera. (This was the only shooting I did against the enemy in the entire war.) A few days later I went to the photo store for the pictures. The salesman said, 'I have to report you to the Gestapo Officer. Do you belong to some kind of underground here? How dare you take pictures of the POWs at the camp. Do you have an explanation?' I did, and he was satisfied, and the whole camp was happy for the Christmas gift they could send from Germany."

"Mr. Haas, with all the bombing and shooting all over the country, you must have been living in a different world," Mr. Wagner said.

"I did, Mr. Wagner, and in some ways I liked it, because I could do a lot of good for those poor fellows." Mr. Wagner was eager to hear everything I had to tell of my life at the camp. "When winter came to the camp, naturally Christmas was on the minds of all the men, both German and French. Even if most of them were not especially religious, at this time of the year something valuable in the old tradition took over the sentiments and the question was, will the Germans allow us to celebrate Christmas here in the camp? As on many occasions, one day Jacque came near me with his biggest smile. I knew something special was coming and I didn't have long to wait. 'Oh, Mr. Haas, we need your help. You know very soon Christmas will be here and we Frenchmen want to have Mass in a nice chapel. But we know also that you cannot build us a chapel here at the camp. We have an idea how it can be done easily and we thought about transforming our big workroom into a nice chapel. We have the right workmen to do this and we have everything else we need—fixtures, electric cables, light bulbs. Everything will be securely installed. We even have a priest to hold the Holy Mass on Christmas Eve at the altar. With your help and the permission of the Commandant we could do it. Will you help us? Wouldn't you like to celebrate Christmas, even in this wartime and in these strange surroundings?'

"That was Jacque. One thing for sure, I had to help, but I thought it wouldn't be as easy as it sounded. The next day I went to the Commandant. I told him the story about the planned Christmas idea in our workroom and waited for an answer. He looked at me for a moment, then said slowly, 'Haas, what an idea. Listen, I have nothing against Christmas, absolutely nothing, but to hold Mass in those wooden barracks, I don't like this idea at all. What about a fire? Those men will set up everything only primitive, and you know yourself how the foundations of the barracks are already deep in snow water. To put some 250 men in this room on Christmas Eve is just inviting big trouble or plain suicide. The barracks will for sure collapse, and then? No, forget this idea. I want to have Christmas in peace, like it should be, don't you?' I didn't leave the office so quickly. 'Mr. Commandant. I have no Christmas vacation. I am not married and I have to stay here at the camp the whole time. I can watch the camp and the whole Christmas business very well and I think I can take the responsibility for this one night.'

"Now the Commandant laughed all over. 'Haas, you poor mouse, your so-called responsibility means absolutely nothing here, don't you know? You will only get me into big trouble and ruin my Christmas vacation with your French celebration on Christmas Eve. But if you will be here the whole time around the barracks and really control the whole thing, in God's name, Haas, I will give my blessing to it. But listen, when I come back from my holiday and your Frenchmen give me trouble, or if something happens at this Christmas business in your workroom, Haas, you will be in jail for a long time!'

"When Christmas Eve came, everything went just fine at the camp. The work was finished by early afternoon. Then the men decorated the normally plain workroom into a Christmas chapel. We planned two meetings for all the men, with about 300 in each. Around 7:00 PM the first group assembled in their own new chapel. For a POW camp, it was the perfect Christmas Eve. Snow covered the ground and all appeared to be very quiet. There was no rushing for anything. The air was cold and the men came slowly with their coat collars up, hands deep in their pockets, huddling together into the warm room. In only a few minutes the whole space was packed like a sardine can. The latecomers had to stand on the benches around the walls. Everybody in the room wanted to see the priest, the Christmas tree, the lights and the improvised altar. Suddenly the sound of a violin playing Silent Night filled the room and as the men became quiet the spirit of Christmas seemed to fill the chapel. Many of those lonely older men appeared as if in a dreamland and in the shadow of the few flickering candles, I saw tears on some of the faces. Others looked like little children. Under the Christmas tree were the gifts provided by the Red Cross, helping the men to forget being in this far-away place in Northern Germany.

"This was an evening of peace, but I wondered when would real peace come? I was still in uniform, which made all the events of the war seem larger and harder. Our troops were now marching around the Mediterranean Sea and heavy bombers came over Germany from England every night, destroying homes and lives of people who were not involved in this war. How long must I remain a soldier? How long will I be in this kind of life?

"With these reflections in mind I almost forgot what I had promised my Commandant a few days ago. Wasn't I responsible for watching over the whole area? Now I needed to get out of the room for a short reconnaissance around the barracks, but how to leave this packed room with so many men jamming the door?

"When I finally got out of the room into the open, the cold wind blew the icy snow right into my face. Strolling around the barracks I thought the Commandant might have been right. The foundations of those wooden buildings were already standing in snow water as if in a swimming pool and the snow reached to the overhanging roof eaves, piling up more and more around the corners of the barracks. The hot air from the hundreds of men inside radiated out like a steam cloud. But, it was Christmas Eve and inside was holy music and celebration and deep joy. To me it looked like the whole barracks was also moving in a joyful Christmas mood.

"While making the second round, I saw something that gave me a start. One side of our barrack was sinking into the water and the front wall was bulging out. My head became hot, then cold; what if the Commandant was right? I would have to stop the meeting at once before the second group, which was already arriving, was ready to start. This was easier thought about than done. Just as the first meeting was ending the second group of men began pushing into the room. It was just too cold to wait outside. I shouted my order trying to stop them, but the heavy wind blew my words away and killed my voice. So I quite trying. I began to pray, 'This is the only joy for these men for a long, long time. May this night not end in a catastrophe; not for them nor for me.' Otherwise it would be a bad Christmas for all of us. To my surprise, the wind stopped at the start of the second meeting, as did the sinking of the barrack into the water. Was I ever glad! I then closed the doors and the meeting later ended without incident. French holy night was over and all was well.

"Early the next morning Jacque and I inspected the area. All around the barrack the sunken posts were deep in water and there was a huge bulge at the front entrance. When the men came to work we put heavy bales on the bulging side of the building and then supported the foundation from the outside and waited to see what the Commandant would say.

"The next day the Commandant came into our camp and immediately saw the trouble spots. He saw the heavy bales on top of the bulging wall and shouted, 'Haas, don't you see? The barracks are sinking into the snow water and the mud. You are out of your mind and you'd better get ready and shift that heavy stuff some other place and away from the ruined entrance.'

"I was saved. I didn't go to jail and there was no catastrophe.

"But some days later, in the middle of the night the fire alarm sounded. The officers' barracks was on fire and the flames burned everything in minutes. We had no time to rescue anything and in a very short time the whole building was only a smoldering ruin; everything had burned and was gone. The day after they discovered that a faulty wire from an electric cooking plate had started the fire, but to our surprise, nobody went to jail. There were always surprises in this world of ours.

"This was a very long winter and life was boring for the POWs in our campground. Naturally Jacque noticed this first and one day I also noticed that there was something new in his head. Beside his ever present smile, he came to me one day with one of his famous opinions. 'Mr. Haas, what do you think about our lonely winter life here at the camp? Isn't it really too boring? Don't you think and feel we could, or we should bring a little more life into our daily routine? The constant monotonous work makes the men stupid. There is nothing else to do but work, work and more work. A little eating and sleeping and it is really a very dull merry-go-round all the time. Some of the men have their own ideas about how to change this situation in a simple and inexpensive way. You see, we have all kinds of men here in the camp. We have good musicians, we have professional athletes, we have singers and entertainers and we thought we should do something with these people. All those men have a very good international background, like the conductor of Maxim Paris and the director of Radio Paris and other such intelligent men. With them we should bring some real life back into their life here. In this way we could do some real good for all of us and everybody would be happy. You know, we thought we should do some show business at the camp; it could be done once a month and we all think it would be fantastic.' I laughed; we both laughed. This new French idea wasn't so bad at all.

Jacque continued, 'Mr. Haas, Sunday is the dullest day in the camp with not much to do the whole day long. But a Sunday show right here once a month would inspire the whole camp life. It would uplift the boring spirit of all our men. Could you think of a better way, and would you like to help us?'

"What could I do in this case? Without the approval of the Commandant I could do nothing. So one day I again went in to see him, telling him of Jacque's new idea about the monthly Sunday show business. When I finished my story about this new idea to uplift the spirits of the POWs I thought this might now be the end of my career at the camp. For some time the Commandant just looked at me with a curious look on his face and then, straightening himself up, he said, 'Haas, have you nothing else to do with your men? Do you think this camp with all these men in it is a private summer resort? Do you think you are here just for a good vacation?' But a grin began to spread over his face. 'Haas, this time you are too late. What you just told me will happen very soon, or right now. Listen, we are building a so-called music hall at the camp ground, just in the middle near the barracks. The instruments are already ordered. Prepare your men and don't forget to make it work like it should.' And so it was. In the very same week the music hall was begun. There was room for about two hundred men with a little stage in front. A few days later I heard the musicians playing and a different look took place on the camp ground. In a few weeks the camp newspaper had an announcement:

Stalag 10C--First Sunday Show--All Free

"I had also been invited and was sitting right in front of the stage between my new friends in POW uniforms, excited like all the others about the new Sunday show. The program began to unfold just like in the entertainment business. It was like a real theater with decorations and a master of ceremonies; artists, singers, musicians, athletes and, of course, comedians. Everything was first class in appearance; very inspiring with lots of noise during the whole evening.

From those first pageants in our new hall I still remember the last event. It was a boxing match, or more accurately, a show boxing match between a Belgian and an English champion. It was exciting. Beside the many French and other POWs, we had also recently received an Englishman in the camp. He was in a special room all alone and had no contact with any of the other men. Why? I never found out. Somehow I learned he was formerly a famous boxing champion in South Wales. There was also a boxing champion from Walloon, Samson the Great. Jacque and I got the idea to bring these two specialists together for one evening. Normally I could not do a thing like that, but on this day the Commandant was not at the camp, and with Jacque I managed the situation. At a sports store in town I borrowed boxing gloves. I told the guard to bring the Englishman out of his cell and into the theater. The rest was up to the POWs and the match could go on. When the curtain opened there was a real boxing ring in front of us. Ropes were strung all around the four corners just like at the pro fights; floodlights above the stage, and when the two men came out I thought the roof would fall in. At the moment the two boxers stood before the people, smiling and laughing at the growing applause, everyone in the hall jumped from their seats and benches shouting and whistling, making a terrible noise. I was almost scared sitting between those wild Frenchmen during all of the five rounds in the ring, but the exciting and thrilling moments continued. The fight ended in a draw. The two men were too tired and just quit. The curtain closed and then the whole room with all those frantic men almost exploded with the thundering noise of shouting and bravos—the first successful Sunday show at Stalag 10C was over.

"When the Commandant returned I had to go to his office. I knew why and was trying to maintain the most innocent face in the world. 'Haas!' the Commandant shouted, 'what in the world is going on here? Who gave you permission to let the Englishman out of his cell? Do you think this is St. Pauli or some amusement park?'

"I said, 'Herr Commandant, the Englishman needed a little exercise. He is always alone in his cell. He got his exercise and it was just fantastic. It was the best medicine for this man and also for all the other POWs in the camp. They all will come back to life and they also want to invite you for the next Sunday show at their theater. It will be a totally different program, and you will surely like it.'

"'Haas, the next show will be when I put you in jail like the poor Englishman! Maybe I will put you two together. But tell me, when will they have the next show?' he asked.

"Usually we practiced for this Sunday show in the barracks between our work hours. I put a guard at the entrance door and we would start singing. There was our first tenor, Leo. He was from Belgium, a man with a brilliant voice. Another fine singer was Ernest, also Charles and others from our group, all with good voices and tones. They sang everything from La Boheme to Rigoletto and it was always a lot of fun.

"One day we got a new Commandant. On his first visit to our workroom he naturally wanted to know what we were doing. After the inspection tour of our rooms and having heard the explanation of the daily routine of the workmen, the Commandant asked me, 'So, and what else is going on here?' I wondered if he already knew that we were doing the Sunday show?

"I said, 'Herr Commandant, besides our daily routine work there is something good going on here. We have a spirit up lifter; we can show you this right here.'

"He was surprised. 'A spirit up lifter? What's that? Do you drink alcohol here?'

"I laughed, 'Oh, no, we don't do things like that, but the intelligence officer taught us singing. The POW men have to learn the German language and singing is a good method for that: a very simple way to teach the Frenchman German. We practice German folk songs and others right here at the camp.'

"'What are you saying, you sing here? I thought you and your men were here to work? I need more explanation.'

"Now I knew the new Commandant was also a good singer, I had heard him once. So I asked, 'Would you like to hear some good songs?' Indeed he would, and then I called Leo out of work and he gave a good rendition of a well known aria.

"'Good,' said the Commandant, 'sing some more. Do you know some parts from Rigoletto?' He gave Leo a tune and Leo nodded and started the song. When the solo part changed to duet style, the Commandant began singing too. Both men stood in the middle of our work room singing Rigoletto with their very good voices. It was just marvelous. Everyone stopped working and the whole room was as quiet as a concert hall. There stood our humble Leo with his poor POW shirt, and beside him the Commandant in his first class uniform, with his hand on the little officer's sword, with both voices blending together in those famous melodies.

"When the song ended the prisoners shouted, 'Bravo, bravo Germany,' and clapped their hands for minutes and jumped up from their seats. In this tumult the Commandant shouted, 'Stop the fun, back to work.' But after he left the room we sang some more, we needed to practice for next Sunday's show.

"Springtime came. All the snow and coldness was suddenly gone, as in an instant. A mild sun was shining over the lonely camp promising some warmer and better days. But for the POWs it was always the same situation, the same kind of life. Some of the young fellows started daydreaming, sitting at their workbenches looking out of the windows and watching the birds flying through the newly greening bushes. Others became sad and started singing love songs as if in better times. It was no wonder. Outside the whole of nature was at freedom. The birds were singing with full joy and nature was coming back to new life. There must be something better than always the stupid work; there must be a world without this daily boring, boring routine. A world without this monotony; a world with something that was always missing here in our prison. We had worked together for almost a year and I too wanted a change somehow, someday.

"Then there was Jacque again in my room, smiling and talking about a new spring problem. 'Mr. Haas, maybe you can help us again with a new problem in our camp life. You know, we have many young men in the camp. They're always behind barbed wires, always alone and maybe forgotten by our folks at home, far away from any girlfriend, nothing for their hearts. Mr. Haas, we have problems with these men, we all have problems, don't you know? We all have almost forgotten how a girl looks. Mr. Haas, is there a way to see girls?'

"'Oh, Jacque, do you think I would smuggle girls into the campground? Or do you think the Commandant might open a girl's camp across the street? Jacque, things like that you'll have to tell the Commandant yourself; this is none of my business.'

"'Oh, Mr. Haas, you've helped us in so many ways, don't you have a way out of this misery? We know you smuggled bread and other things into the camp, but don't think wrong of us, we don't want to get you into trouble with the Commandant; no, we just want so see some girls, that's all.' So that was the new problem, seeing girls. But it was a knotty problem. I had to fix this without the Commandant's knowledge, otherwise I would be in big trouble.

"Then I had an idea. I needed to pick up a few parcels from the post office in town and would use the camp's big truck. I put a few of the men inside the truck, closed the curtain, leaving just enough room for them to peak through to see the outside world and drove through the gate and into town. My, did the fellows in the back of the truck have a good time. They forgot camp and the workroom. While we drove up and down the streets my friends looked out to see the Frauleins walking on the streets. This must have been a lot of fun. The girls walked around in the sunshine and the poor POWs smiled happily. I stopped at the post office and everyone got out unto the street. This was another nice part of our excursion. Then Jacque discovered a nice looking girl coming straight toward him. He said to her, 'Ooh, la la, mein Fraulein.'

"The girl quickly recognized his uniform as being from the camp nearby and answered quickly, 'Ooh, la la, bonsoir monsieur.' Jacque became electrified. What a beautiful life it was outside the camp. We all laughed. The girl disappeared and Jacque felt so lonely again. On the way back to camp Jacque complained, 'Oh, Mr. Haas, why must we go back so fast, back to the dull camp? Here outside is the finest sunshine, here is life; what a terrible life we are in. When will the war be over? I want to be home and walk with my Madeleine on the Promenade. She is waiting in Paris all this time. Here I wait also and just hang around doing nothing. What nonsense is war.'

"'Jacque, I don't know when this war will be over, maybe soon, maybe not, who knows? We all want to go home and be out of this war misery. Someday you will be back home in Paris, strolling along the Seine Promenade with your girl friend, happy again and forgetting all those days at the camp. You must just wait; that's the soldier's fate all over the world.'

"But, the war was not over soon. It just took different directions for us, and when summertime came, my time at Stalag 10C was also coming to an end. I was transferred to another division which then received orders to go to Norway. There began my new adventure and soon I forgot the camp and all the work in the wooden barracks fenced all around with the barbed wires. With my new comrades I boarded a ship in Denmark and was soon en route to Norway, far, far away from home and also far, far away from the end of the war."

"Mr. Haas, I'm glad I am on this ship, otherwise I wouldn't know the other side of the war."

"Soon we will be in New York. Now you will have to tell me some of your stories," I replied.

"I will, but you should know that your war is over, you are out of it. I am still in it for the rest of my life. I have to win people over to Christ and this is a hard warfare too. This coming Sunday I will hold church services right here on deck for all the people on the ship. People have to know where they are going. Too many only go to America to seek a richer life and go after the almighty dollar and forget the real life. We Christians too often are too shy or too timid to tell others of our wonderful new life with Christ in this world. Do you know the new song 'Power in the Blood?' We will sing it and we all should learn it by heart. There is no better way for this world today."

Usually in the afternoon I would sit in the salon to meet other people. We had about forty first-class passengers on board and I did a lot of talking with two of them. I wanted to learn better English in spite of the fact that they were also of German origin. One day I overheard an interesting conversation between these two fellows. Both came from New York; one was a doctor, the other a grocery store owner. The doctor said, "Have you seen how many emigrants are on the boat? There must be at least 900 to 1,000. And they are all on their way to Paradise, or that is what they think America is. I am afraid they will have a bad surprise when they are on land. It is even hard for me to make a decent living now. How is it with your grocery store?"

"I closed my store for two weeks," the grocer said. "I needed a vacation too and I went back to the small island where I was born. There I dedicated my hotel. You know, everybody needs a nest egg for later on in life. Now I'm going back to work making more sauerkraut and potato salad." They both laughed.

The doctor asked, "What do you want to do for the coming holidays? Why not take a short vacation in Bermuda? I read an advertisement, $500 for the weekend. That's a bargain today. Should we go together?"

"Oh, boy. The holidays are my best money days. I too have to work very hard these days. We sent too many packages to the poor folks at home. I think I will let you know about it later. In the meantime I have to make lots of potato salad."

"And sauerkraut," added the doctor and we all laughed. But I thought that if these two fellows from New York can go for a mini vacation for $500 to Bermuda, then I will survive too. They don't have it so bad, they didn't look very poor to me.

On another day I was sitting in the salon at the coffee table. While playing chess with another passenger a man came to our table. I didn't know if he was one of the first-class Americans or one of the poor emigrants. But while sitting there, he took off his shoes and put his feet right on the table. Now I knew he was a real American because I had seen this behavior by the U.S. soldiers after the war at the Spa Promenade in Wiesbaden. For us Europeans, this was something very strange. But here at our table nobody said a word; everybody just stared toward the feet of the new fellow. Minutes later my wife came into the salon and came straight to our table. While sitting beside me she looked the fellow over and said nothing. After about a minute a miracle happened. The feet went down from the table, he put his shoes back on and everybody smiled, including the new American. Why these fellows have to put their shoeless feet on coffee tables in a public place, I still don't know.

In a few minutes, out of the blue sky the two swinging doors flew wide open and a terrible wind blew into the salon.

The whole place started to move like an earthquake. The piano jumped out of the jacks and all the dishes slid from one corner to another. The violinist in the little band clamped his violin under his arm and disappeared from the room. A sailor shouted, "We have a storm coming, everybody must return to their room." What a surprise. But going to our room was not easy. The boat was swaying all over and everyone looked like drunkards gliding over the deck. The storm became stronger, about grade eleven, blowing just off Newfoundland. I'd never been in a situation like that. The first day I wasn't affected very much. Standing on the top deck I thought the boat would completely disappear into the wild ocean. Deep into the water, then very high into the black air, rolling around so violently until nearly everyone on board was seasick.

At supper nobody went into the dining room except my three year old Erika who announced, "Daddy, I'm hungry." What could I do? I went up near the kitchen, near to the smell of the food and it was terrible for me.

The waiter asked her, "Aren't you seasick?"

"No, I want to eat," she said.

"You are a very brave girl, I will serve you the whole menu." Which he did. I had to sit there until Erika slowly consumed soup, potatoes and so on until the end of the complete meal. We again passed close to the terrible smell of the kitchen on the swaying deck. I was amazed—the little children did not get seasick at all and at the kindergarten on deck they were all having a very good time. The rest of the passengers suffered for three days. Then, as suddenly as the storm had appeared, it disappeared. When we found ourselves suddenly sailing along Long Island, the sea was as calm as in a picture, and there was no hint of the terrible storm we'd passed through.

But in bed at night I noticed something else. There was a terrible smell all over and it was coming from the outside. The next day a sailor said, "Oh, this is normal. We are coming into New York and this is the smell of perfume from the big city." It was in the water, the oil, the dirt and whatever humans put into the water, nobody could take it out. So it was finally the last night on the ship after twelve days from Bremerhaven to New York, this part of the adventure now coming to an end. We sailed into the harbor of New York at night and would be on land the next day.

In the darkness I stood at the railing and looked toward New York. That was a view! The air was so clear it was just a wonderful picture of a gigantic city. And the lights—lights and lights all over. From the left side the street lights went into a never ending direction and on the right side the city looked the same. Some low clouds were sailing right in front of the huge buildings high up in the dark sky. What an impressive picture for my first sight of America. I stood there looking and looking, then I became aware of what would happen the next day. How would I survive in this great land, a land with a different culture, language and many other things that I didn't know about? At this moment somebody stood beside me; it was the missionary from Seattle. He put his arm around my shoulders and said, "Mr. Haas, don't be afraid, you will make it. You are a Christian and a German and you have a profession. You will not be alone in this new land. Others have done it and you can do it also. Just have courage and trust in the Almighty Lord." This was great support and I felt better toward the unknown future. Behind me on the ship in the huge dance hall full of noise, some emigrants had spent their last money in drinking and dancing and having a great time. Tomorrow would be another new day and for me the discovery of America would start right then and there.

America

"Gertrud, this is America, we made it!" After twelve long days we had sailed from Bremerhaven to Hoboken, New Jersey.

After disembarking from the ship we stood on the pier of Hoboken right in the middle of the crowd of immigrants. Then an older couple with a rolled magazine in hand came toward us.

"Welcome to America, you must be the Haas family."

"Yes, we are and you must be Mr. and Mrs. Wasenmiller from Philadelphia?" We all smiled and shook hands. "Now you've made it to the promised land, just head for the customs inspection and we can go."

I had never gone through a customs inspection and had no time to prepare. The inspector couldn't wait for me to open my package, he just tore it apart. With all his inspection he found nothing wrong with the contents.

As he discovered my wife's guitar, he asked, "Oh, would you like to sell this musical instrument here?"

"No, no, this is an old guitar, my mother gave it to me when I was still very young."

"An old guitar? Do you know that old musical instruments are very valuable? You may have to pay duty. What did you pay for it?" he wanted to know.

"I paid nothing, it was gift from my mother," Gertrud explained.

"How do I know it is yours? Can you play?"

"Play right now?" Gertrud wondered anxiously. "What should I play?"

"Well, play something, I have to know," he insisted.

Gertrud was now really shocked. But, in the midst of this crowd she started playing and singing the hymn, *Grosser Gott Wir Lieben Dich*. When she started the second stanza the inspector shouted, "Stop! This is enough. Pack your stuff together, you may go." Without inspecting any of our other items he gave me the papers and we were allowed to go.

Some others were not so lucky. The man beside me had a big wooden box. He had to open it and take out all his china; he had many, many pieces which he put all on the floor of the pier. But we were driven with our new sponsors in two cars away from the harbor and pier and into the land of my dreams. But right away, my good dreams were shattered. The streets looked so strange. Very high weeds were in the streets. The houses were not like those in Germany and the kids in the streets made fun of the old people by throwing old cardboard boxes at them. What a surprise. But Mr. Wasenmiller said, "You will see better things, this too will change in the future."

After driving about three hours into New Jersey we crossed a huge bridge over the Delaware River into a town. The driver said, "Now we are in Philadelphia, this will be your future hometown."

I looked around in disbelief and said, "Oh, this couldn't be Philadelphia."

Mr. Wasenmiller laughed, "How do you know? You've never been here, how can you say this isn't Philadelphia?"

I remembered reading books with pictures of Philadelphia. Places with great buildings and business sections, but this part of town was anything but a great city. I said again, "No, this cannot be the real Philadelphia, these small places and buildings are not yet finished, they don't even have roofs on top."

Mr. Wasenmiller was quiet for awhile, then he laughed and laughed about my remarks. "Oh, you miss the German roofs? I'll have to explain it to you. You need to know we have a lot of storms like hurricanes here, so the houses all have flat roofs so the strong winds can't blow the top of the houses away; we don't need German gables here."

It was still strange to me, but it made sense. How did I know what a real hurricane was? We stopped in a small street and went into our first U.S. apartment. It was quite different from the houses in Germany, but everything was clean and filled with furniture, and ready to move into. Mr. Wasenmiller said, "Everything you see here in this room is yours and the rent for the month will be $45.00. There is nothing else for you to pay and we wish you all the best in your new country."

I had heard of other immigrant's fate; they had to work and pay for two or three years until the first expenses were paid off. Mr. Wasenmiller was reading my mind. "Don't worry, our church members and other friends gave all this for you absolutely free. They have enough themselves and will be happy that you have a good beginning in Philadelphia." That was just too much for me. I felt like a king after my poor life in Germany after the war. Now I could live in a two bedroom apartment alone with my family. It was unbelievable.

Everything was paid for right at the beginning in the new land. I knew that I must write to my mother about this the next day; she has to know how real Americans are. What a great country and good people. When the Wasenmillers left, I almost danced around with Gertrud. You have to experience this. Since my wedding about seven years before I had never lived alone in an apartment. My family always had only one room on the same floor with my mother-in-law, sister-in-law, grandmother and landlord. And we all had to use one toilet, one kitchen and there was no bath. But now—now I had everything, even a bathroom. Wow! Now I was really alone with my little family; it seemed unbelievable!

Our first night in Philadelphia was certainly different from the bunk beds on the boat. Now we slept in civilized beds until 8:00 in the morning when Gerhard ran into our bedroom shouting, "Daddy, Daddy, you have to come. There is a black lady who wants to talk to you." I thought, what is going on? I went into the living room and behind a window a black lady was smiling broadly and wanted to talk to me. But I couldn't open the window, not with all my tricks; it seemed to be nailed down on all corners. Then we both gave up our first U.S. conversation. Later I asked the landlord about those funny windows. With a fast turn of a switch he opened it. "Yes," he said with a smile, "this is a U.S. window, you don't see them in Germany? Just up and down, you will like it."

And we did. We learned many new things here, and the next new thing was the heating system. My landlord was a dentist who lived outside the city. To get heat, he had to be up very early turning on the oil heater in the basement. He said if I wanted to do it he would give me $5.00 off my rent. Naturally I did it; at this time $5.00 was good money, easily earned. Almost immediately I ran into my first trouble. This house had four stories and the two heating pipes went straight along my bedroom wall up to the next floor. After sleeping about two hours the wall behind our bed became so hot it was almost impossible to sleep and I had to work the next day. Then I found a quick solution. Outside on the floor was the thermostat for the whole house. When the room got too hot I just went out and turned the thermostat down and my room cooled off quickly. Now we could sleep easily again. But two hours later the room became hot again. What was going on? I went out and turned it down again, waiting to see what went wrong with the thing. Instantly from the upper floor I heard foot steps tap, tapping down the stairs. I stood in a dark corner and saw an elderly lady coming down. She turned the heater up again. Then she spotted me. We were both in pajamas. She shouted at me, "Don't you do it again, do you think we want to freeze upstairs? We pay our rent like you and we want heat in this cold weather. Do you think we should die upstairs? You better learn to manage the American way you F.O.B man," and up the stairs she went. I was curious, what kind of a man is an F.O.B. Man?

The next morning I asked the dentist about it and he laughed. "Don't take it so seriously, what can I do? It's an old house and the lady is partially right. In this country we have to adjust. Maybe you should turn your bed around and that might solve the problem. About the F.O.B. man," he laughed again, "it means 'Fresh off the boat'—that's what you are, the newcomers."

We lived one block from the famous Girard Avenue. On the corner was a huge ten story stone building that looked like a factory. I asked a neighbor what kind of factory or office building it was, but he only laughed. "This is not a factory, it is something much better, it is a hospital."

"My, a hospital?" I wouldn't want to be in this cement block; no park nearby, no garden, no greenery or benches for recovering or relaxing, no trees or fresh air, how could it be a hospital? "But this is America," I thought.

Across the street was the Jewish open market, a totally different world for us. Here one could buy live animals. Chicken and fish were cut right before your eyes, ready to take home, and you could always make a good deal by bargaining. In most windows a sign said, "We speak all languages." It was no wonder, with Yiddish you can go through the whole world and most of these fellows came from the old country, or the European border states. They could easily have learned three or four languages in their childhood. In one clothing store was the sign "We don't sell cheap clothes, we sell good clothes cheap." When pedestrians weren't in the mood to buy there was a strong salesman who pulled you right into the store for another bargain. It worked most of the time and you could buy seven days a week and even at Christmas time; stores were open all night. This was also America.

Learning English was my first real job and the best way was at the work place. Find a good job and people will teach you all that you need. But in many places the workers want to improve their old German speaking skills and when they discovered I was from Germany, they all wanted to speak in German to me. That didn't help me much. I was a fine custom tailor but many people didn't know about such stores in Philadelphia. I looked through the newspaper for something in this line and found a temporary job repairing clothing at a cleaning plant. At least I had a job making some money and a good man there to teach me English. It was the job foreman who was a giant of a man with the heart of a good boy. He was Black Jimmy. I could come any time for questions in English or about explanations of the written work orders; he always had time for me and we worked well together. It was about eight weeks before Christmas when I was working in the morning when all of a sudden I heard some Christmas songs in German in our workroom. Across from my work place was the pressing department and about ten men, all black, were laughing and singing and pressing all at the same time. They were a happy bunch of people and I asked Jimmy what was going on. But Jimmy was laughing too. "Jimmy, what's the singing about? It's still six weeks until Christmas, are those fellows all mixed up?"

He still laughed, "You are right, but you don't know. Those guys are not mixed up. Most of them were in WW II in Germany and they learned those songs in Germany and today they just wanted to do you a favor. They know you are German, that's all."

Then I went to them and said, "Danke Schoen."

Then they shouted back, "Ja wohl, Ja wohl, mein Herr."

Another day I had to pack finished clothing, especially fine dresses for sending out of the plant to customers. When taking the hangers from the rack I got almost a shock. Right on the top of the big hanging rack I saw great dark creatures, large, like little fingers marching along the whole rack. I called, "Jimmy! Jimmy, see what's jumping all around these dresses! This is all expensive stuff, maybe I packed these animals into the boxes too?"

But Jimmy only laughed. "Don't be afraid, these are common German roaches, don't you know?"

"Jimmy, these creatures I never saw in Germany—never— you are wrong."

Jimmy said, "I know, don't be scared; see these little rascals here," and he caught one with his fingers and started to hand it to me, "See, a long time ago they came from China on a boat and now they are all over the city and we can't get rid of them. When you see one again, just shake it off the rack and put your foot on it and that will be the end of the jumping fellow."

We also had a night watchman with a huge dog. When I came into the job one morning the dog was resting in the middle of a large box full of dresses which were to be cleaned. I ran to Jimmy complaining about the sleeping dog on top of the fine dresses in the box. But Jimmy with his usual broad smile just said, "You Germans just need a little more heart, don't you know how cold it is outside the building in Philadelphia? This poor fellow was watching the whole night, he needs a good rest."

My work was only temporary; I was replacing another workman who was on a three month vacation in California. When he came back I had to look for another job. From the newspaper I found another notice for one at an address in downtown Philadelphia. At lunchtime I went to the banking section of the city on Chestnut Street, to the sixteenth floor across from City Hall. I took the elevator up and when the door opened I was standing right in front of the finest clothing store in all Philadelphia. What a surprise! The whole floor was occupied by a men's clothing business with a huge work room.

When I talked to the boss he offered me a wage which was not very high, "See young fellow, the grass is only greener on the other side; we don't pay much, but better than you are making now. You must understand, you are totally new here in Philadelphia. You will have to learn much in our fine city store. You still have a long way to go to get rich in the USA." I needed the money so I took the job and they were happy I did because they were loaded with work.

My work place was at a huge window and one day I saw a man's face appearing from the outside—on the sixteenth floor? How did the man get there? My co-worker explained. "They are cleaning the windows from the outside, lowering a huge board from the top doing their risky business every day." My co-worker continued, "Did you ever hear of the great depression? It was about 1930 to 1934 and many strange things happened at that time in the USA. In this neighborhood a rich man owned almost the whole street—twelve houses. But when the depression came and hit Philadelphia too, none of his houses were paid for. He could not repay the original owner and lost all of it. Overnight he became a poor man and it was too much for him. He couldn't take it and saw no way out of his dilemma so he went up to the sixteenth floor window and just jumped. That was his end. Can you understand?"

I couldn't. I said, "My, you live here in a Christian country, and certainly he was a Christian, how could he do this strange thing? There is in life always a solution, even if he was not a good Christian, no matter how grave the situation might be."

My main problem was learning English. Back home in Germany my sister was learning English in school. She wrote to me, "Learning English is no big problem. The grammar is very easy to learn and when you listen to how people speak you will soon have it." But the theory and practice are very different. In German you speak like you write, but in English it is very different. Another problem was that in every store there were men who wanted to brush up on their old German language. Even in this store there was an older man from Hungary who spoke some German but always wanted to improve it through me. Then another man gave me a totally new suggestion on how to learn English the best way. He said, "It is very easy, if you don't understand what people are saying, just smile back and say, "Yes, yes."

I used this method for quite awhile with some success until I came upon the wrong person. This fellow asked me a strange question I didn't understand, but I smiled and instantly said, "Yes, yes." When he saw my reaction he became overly excited.

He shouted, "You—you understand absolutely nothing of English. If you wanted to know what I just now asked you, you would be ashamed and be running away fast." So I gave up this method of learning English and went back to my dictionary to learn vocabulary.

On the subway every morning I always saw an elderly man sitting across from me. I used the time studying my dictionary and the man watched me. One day he said to me, "Mr., you must be a very religious man." I was surprised. I didn't know this man and how could he know from the outside if I was a very religious man?

"How do you know?" I asked.

"Oh, this is very easy to see. You read your Bible every morning right here on the subway," he replied.

I smiled, "Sir, this is not a Bible, it is just an English dictionary. I am new here in the country and have to learn the language fast. I must use it in my business."

"Wonderful, wonderful," he said, "then we can talk together more and maybe I can teach you more English too." But this was not so easy for me. Listening and talking in a new language are two very different things. I found out very soon what the practice was.

For Christmas my son wanted a yoyo. On the way home from work I went into a drugstore for a yoyo. But the man didn't understand my words so I tried to demonstrate right in the store what a real yoyo was. "See," I tried to explain, "a yoyo is a thing that will fly right up into the air. You have to use two sticks with a string together and the yoyo with his two heels will fly up and then you have to catch it before it falls to the ground." The man watched my movements with some astonishment, then looked at me as if totally mixed up about my English and raised his hands toward me and pushed me out of his store.

"Sir, please never come back. Get out of my store." he ordered. Out I went on the street wondering what was wrong with my explanation. Then I realized that I had said heels for wheels and I went back into the store. "Sir, I made a mistake, the yoyo doesn't have two heels it has two wheels."

But the man shouted this time, "Didn't I tell you never to come back into my store? I don't care if your yoyo has two heels or two wheels or ten wheels. Out! Out or I'll call the police!"

Out I went again, but on my way home I found another drugstore and in the window I saw my yoyo. I went in and asked the salesman for it. "Oh, yes, we have those. Do you know how to use it? Should I demonstrate it?" he asked. Then I told him the story of my experience with the other drugstore and we both laughed. "Say, where did you learn your good English? I understood you right away because I am German too." Now I had my yoyo for $2.00 and Gerhard had his Christmas present.

Another method of learning English the more easy way was by watching TV. This idea came from a neighbor who had tried this system before me. So we bought a used TV for $38.00 and it was just wonderful. Every evening the whole family watched TV news and all the reporters with their excellent speaking ability. We used all the funny movements, facial expressions, especially when you have to learn the tongue movements. Saying the "th" wasn't so easy; you have to be a real tongue twister flexing the tongue around like a snake from the bottom to the top of the mouth and hissing the tone out of the mouth; upstairs, downstairs, looking and sounding like a handicapped fellow. How somebody could invent a language like that is still a mystery to me. But we had to learn it. The kids didn't care much for TV learning, they were learning it easily on the street from the other kids faster than we did. But they did watch Zorro and Davy Crockett which was more interesting than the news reporter. These were the great hero guys at that time and the console TV was a great Christmas gift. Until the day came when we thought we were doing too much TV watching. We had to do something to stop so much watching. One day help came. The TV broke and the repair cost too much so we stopped watching TV altogether.

It was my first Christmas time in Philadelphia. After work at 6:00 P.M. I walked toward the subway station. The streets were full of people, all rushing home from one side of the street to the other. Only the traffic lights stopped the rush for a minute and the people stood like human walls on each side of the street ready to race to the other side. We stood there like sardines in a can and I was right in the middle of it all. Nobody moved. But beside me an old grandma just couldn't wait for the green light. Then I heard two ladies talking together. They spoke in my Hessian dialect; it was like music to my ears. The younger said, "Oma, stop running, the light has to change first, then we will go over to the other side."

I couldn't hold my tongue, "Oma, Oma, you have time, we all want to go over to the other side, this is America." Like lightning, Oma looked at me expecting to see a ghost or something, not somebody from her home town right here on Chestnut Street in all the hubbub before Christmas Eve.

"Where do you come from?" she asked.

Then the light changed and as the human wall ran over I shouted, "Oma, have a merry Christmas!" We all disappeared into the running mass of people and I saw her no more. Things like that happened, these are the happy surprises of many people in all ways of life.

Back home we celebrated a solemn German Christmas Eve. We lit our little Christmas tree with real candles from Germany; we read the story of Christ's birth from St. Luke in the Bible and sang some familiar songs from home. Gertrud played the guitar and we had a nice warm room, enough to eat and we all had little gifts around the tree. What else did we need? We were all happy. I had a good job and our American adventure had a good beginning. Certainly we missed the second holiday as is the custom in Germany, but this is America, it is different.

After only one day of official Christmas celebration, I went back to my work place. My boss was sitting at the entrance and called me over to him. "See, Kurt, you remember I hired you with the promise of a steady job. That was before Christmas and we really were very busy. But now, Christmas is over and the work is slowing down. I have to care for seven other fellows who are union members and I can't lay them off. I'm so sorry I have to tell you that you will be out of work. You are not a union member so I have to let you go, but what can I do? You are a good man and surely you'll find a good job again. Philadelphia is a big city with many opportunities for the right man. I wish you good luck." There it was. Now it was after Christmas and no work. Out on the street I was afraid to go home and tell Gertrud the bad news. What would she say?

But Gertrud was brave. She said plainly, "Then I have to go to work. You can look after the kids after school and I will find a job somewhere." And she did. She did cleaning in a bakery store. Despite being a professional nurse from Germany, she could not find a job in her field as she was not an American citizen yet. Very often she had Erika with her at the job, using the subway and street car with her broken English language, coming home in the evening very tired. Our American adventure seemed to be turning out exactly as the English teacher back in Germany had said, "The first year of being an immigrant is terrible, the second year is also hard to get over and the third year you get used to it because you have to, there is no way out."

Then another unexpected event happened in our new life. Gerhard came down with whooping cough and Erika was sick with a skin rash. Then she caught the whooping cough also. It was terrible, the two kids coughed all the time, day and night. It became worse and I thought it would never stop. What could we do? We tried all our home remedies but nothing worked. We had to see a doctor. But out of work and with almost no money, no health insurance (in America there was no health insurance like we had in Germany), yet something had to be done. In the evening we were sitting at the bedside of the kids (we put them together), Gertrud said almost crying. "This is just too much for me. You have no work, the kids have this terrible sickness and we have no relatives at all in this country. Why did we come here? I'm afraid to tell you. I'd like to go home to my mother; she will have some solution and can help us. Let's start all over again back home and forget America. It's not what I expected. It's just too hard for me, and for you too."

"Gertrud, we can't go back. (She was just about at the end of her rope.) We can't go home like nothing happened the last time. You know we have no money to do this. How will we buy a new home? Or even a small apartment? Or to start a business again? If we give up now we will be worse off than when we came in the beginning; even worse than just after the war. No, Gertrud, we can't go back. You will see it will be better some day after the winter is gone. First the kids have to get better and then the world will look better for you too."

Then a friend told us of a Dr. Pepper, a doctor of German descent who often helped poor German immigrants without a fee. I thought, I'll see him tomorrow. (When his mother had come from Germany a long time ago she had told him that if he saw poor German immigrants who were new to the country to help them for free, convinced that they were also having a hard time getting started as she had.) When I met Dr. Pepper I told him about the terrible whooping cough problem my two bedridden children had. He was very friendly and promised to come right over after his hospital rounds that evening. He did and he was very serious about the situation with the sickness. After giving them medicine he promised to come back later which he did, and even later again at night. He even came early in the morning, looked at the kids and then said, "The kids will come through. I will come later this afternoon to see the improvement." He did and when I wanted to pay him he said, "No, you pay me only for the medicine, $2.00, and if you need me again, let me know."

What a good doctor! What a blessing for us newcomers; and this was also America.

One day Gertrud's boss asked her, "Say, Gertrud, what is your husband doing these days?"

"At the moment he is out of work, even though he's a good craftsman. The season is over now after Christmas and in the wintertime, who will now give him work? He is also not a union member, so it isn't so easy," she explained.

"Oh, Gertrud, don't worry, there is always a way in America out of a crisis. I have a good friend in our lodge and he is the foreman in a fine store here in Philadelphia. I will talk with him about your husband." The next day he told her, "Send your husband to Frank, the foreman of the shop, he may have a solution."

What a change so quickly. Someone had told me that here in America, "You can learn anything in just three months and, when you have the Pope as a friend, you need only one month to find the right job." Now, I didn't have the Pope as a friend, so would I find a job next week?

I met Frank the next day and he asked me, "Are you a real tailor and not just a gasoline tailor who just cleans pants and cuts trousers?" I showed him my professional papers from Germany and after some more talk he told me I could start working the next Monday, even without being a union member. For some time I didn't know what a "tschoonien" member was until I finally learned it was just a worker's organization. Then I learned about the union business. Four weeks later the union boss came in person to our work place for an inspection. When he discovered me, a total stranger in the store, he shouted, "Who in the world let you work here in this place? You have to leave right away. The only man who has a right to bring you into this place is me, do you understand?"

What could I do? I was hired by Frank and so I told him to talk to Frank. He and Frank talked together for sometime like old buddies and afterward the frightful talk of the union boss calmed down and I didn't have to leave. I worked in this store for three more years and I liked it there.

One of the fellow workers in the shop was Alexander, an older man who wanted to teach me English the easiest way. He said, "Kurt, I want to teach you the three most important words in the English language."

"Alexander, what are they?" I asked.

"Listen," said Alexander, "the three most important words in the English language are 'Take it Easy.'" I laughed.

Frank, who stood nearby must have heard some of our conversation because he called me to his desk and asked, "What did Alexander tell you?"

I said, "He just taught me the three most important words in the English language."

"And what did he teach you?" he asked.

I explained, "Alexander said that the three most important words in the English language are 'Take it Easy.'"

Now Frank laughed too. Then he said, "That's just like old Alexander, he is the laziest man in the store and he will never learn. For ten years he sits in the same place, never improving, but Kurt, with this idea you will never get ahead in America. Listen, if you want to get ahead in our store or in America, you must learn my two most important words in the English language."

"Frank, what are they," I asked.

Then Frank said in a very official tone, "My two most important words in the English language are 'Hurry Up!'" Now I laughed too, but I never forgot this lesson and to this day I am still thankful for that advice from Frank.

On the whole, Frank was a very correct boss. Before I started working for him he said, "You have to start work Monday morning at 8:30 sharp. Or better yet, you must be sitting at your place five minutes early. You get paid for eight hours and you have to work eight hours also. When you are ten minutes late, your pay check on Friday will be docked half an hour." Some weeks we weren't so busy and I had to take a day off in the middle of the week. Then Frank came to my work place to tell me, "Kurt, tomorrow you have to stay home, we don't have enough work for you."

But when Frank wasn't there the secretary, Edith, had to give me the message. When she came to my place, she always said, "Kurt, tomorrow you will have a holiday, isn't that nice?" What a difference in giving an unpleasant message.

The store, Strawbridge and Clothier, was one of the finest in Philadelphia. The subway had a station directly in front of the store and in bad weather we did the best business. We also had one of the first credit cards in America and I could have stayed employed there for life. But later I went out on my own because I wanted to make more money. But it turned out to be a big mistake.

After a short time there I met Martha, another co-worker in the store. She was very friendly, but when she found out I came from Germany she seemed to go wild. With her two balled fists she came over to me and shouted, "You, you should be burned, you and all of your Germany should be burned in hell!" She was really upset with me. What a situation I was running into. What could I do? I said nothing. I was never a Nazi and I was shocked.

When she calmed down I said in my Hessian dialect (Martha was from Frankfurt, not far from my hometown),

"Martha, if the whole of Germany should be burned down, right away another 32,000 of your people will have to die too."

She looked at me again and said slowly, "No, I don't want to do this thing, it has to stop, forever. But you know it was too hard for me all those long years afterwards. I will tell you later."

This was her story: Martha was the only survivor of her entire family in Frankfurt; all the others were lost in those hard years under the Nazi regime (only after the war ended had I too learned the ultimate fate of the Jewish people). Her parent's fine home in Frankfurt was destroyed by the bombing. Somehow she escaped to France and after the war she came to America, now working as a seamstress in our store. In spite of all the misery in Germany she still had in mind to someday go home and visit the old country. In her Hessian dialect she said, "Kurt, I still want to go home for a short visit to our former place in Frankfurt. You know, I would go in the evening when nobody would see me. I want to go over to Kaiser Strasse around the Eschenheimer Tower right into the Friedberger Allee where my father's house was. I was born there and I know every tree around there. Then I would pass my hands over the remaining stones and trees and then I would go slowly back to the airport. I just want to be there once again before I die." With a handkerchief she wiped some tears from her eyes and felt like a little child without father or mother or anyone. Then she said, "Kurt, I must look silly, but I cannot help it, sometimes I feel like that." Many times later we talked about our time back home in Germany before the terrible war started remembering what a nice life we had over there. We became good friends and our Hessian dialect was an invisible bridge covering the bad things in the past.

My landlord was a nice fellow, but I wanted to move out of this place which was close to the slums of Philadelphia. There was no playground for the kids; they played between the parked cars on the dusty street. Most immigrants started here in this cheap area and once they were better established they moved away to one of the better sections of the city. I found a better apartment to the north and the day I was packing and getting ready to move a white lady came around to talk to me. I knew her from talking with her before but today she was really in deep emotion.

She almost cried and said, "Mr. Haas, why do you want to go away so fast? You have been here only three months. I just found out you are from the Rhine area and I too come from the Rhine at Cologne. When you are gone I will miss you very much because there is nobody here to talk to in my language and I feel lost in Philadelphia. You know I married a U.S. soldier back home and everything looked so nice, but now I have to live all the time with strange folks. I am homesick. I can't move away from here even if I wanted to. I have to stay here the rest of my life, alone, without my folks back home and maybe I'll never see them again. Oh, don't move away. I'd like to talk to you once in awhile. Maybe I made a big mistake by marrying this man, but I just loved him when he was in Germany and he is still good to me, but it's all so different here. Oh, my mother told me all this before, but what could I do? Now I am here."

"Yes," I replied, "it's not easy to move into an unknown country with different ideas and life styles. But there are also good people around who will understand you. Why don't you look for a church connection? I did the same thing and my church is a big help, not for money, but just for living together and carrying our burdens in this hard life." When she said goodbye she was still crying, but promised me that she would be a good wife and would learn to adjust to the new people here.

Philadelphia, Paul Street

Now we lived in a better place, farther north from the tough south area. There was even a school right across the street for the kids. There the kids learned English faster than we did without any outside help. We had a small garden and around the corner was a nice playground and park. It was really good and we liked it better than the old place on Franklin Street. But after ten days I discovered a new worm in the nice apple. My new landlord was a happy widow with a Polish friend and every weekend they got together for party time above our rooms. After 7:00 PM the old gramophone was playing wild music and they were dancing Polish polkas. For the whole evening the house was shaking and I was afraid the ceiling would fall down at any minute. They jumped and they stomped, always full of alcohol. Then Gerhard said, "Daddy, at the old house we had the heat problem, now we have this wild dancing business every weekend, what will be next?"

"Next? Next, Gerhard, next we will buy a house for ourselves, then we will be the landlord and can do whatever we want to do," I said.

"A house? Daddy, are we buying a new house? You must be dreaming. We don't even have a car like everybody else has," he pointed out.

"Don't you know we live in America? Here everything is possible, you just have to think in that direction." I told him.

"But Daddy, please don't buy a house like Mr. Krachtus has, that would be too primitive. He just owns a tower house, one room above the other." Our good friend Krachtus and his whole family were from German Romania and they now lived in a house that he called 'My Palace.' A few weeks prior he had invited us to see his house in old Philadelphia and we were really surprised by this ancient building.

At the door we stepped right into the first room and Mrs. Krachtus said, "Welcome, won't you look at our special place? This is Room #1, we call it the multipurpose room. We have a kitchen, living room and dining room, all in one combination. Please follow me." She opened a wall papered door that we didn't see at first and behind it was the staircase upstairs. From above hung a long rope. We all clung to the rope and climbed the spiral steps up to Room #2. On this second floor was the bedroom for the parents. Then, one person at a time, we followed the hanging rope up to Room #3. There was another room, one on top of the other and we went into the bedroom of a boy, then into the bedroom of the girl. Going back down wasn't easy; winding around and around, always with hands on the hanging rope until we landed again in the kitchen. This was the way many of the old pioneers had to live until they could afford better housing. Karl Krachtus wanted to do the same thing. He was a builder, a good worker and saved all his money for a new house. After three years he bought five acres of land in New Jersey and built his dream house, but then a few years later he was worn out. After a heart attack, from which he never fully recovered, he wasn't able to enjoy his new dream house for very long. When I attended his funeral I remember thinking about the hard part of life in America, and death. What is life without eternal hope? Always running after something better and then you have to go—but this is America too.

All immigrants were running into the same trap. They soon learn the American dream, enjoy freedom and live in their own home. I was no exception and had the same idea. To move ahead the best way how, keeping on working, saving your money and then buying a house. When an Italian businessman looked for a helper I went to work in the evening after my regular work day. That was my second job, from 6 to 10 PM, three days a week. But then another businessman needed a helper to work on Sundays. I took it and worked from 10 to 4 PM. Then another of my neighbors came looking for a helper to distribute newspapers, so for three months, from 5:30 AM until 8 AM I did it. That was something different for me. But I had heard that every millionaire in America started out as a newspaper boy! I didn't want to be a millionaire but I felt good and if I could make an extra dollar, why not?

Before the newspaper work we went to a café for an early breakfast. It was 4:30 AM and many times the snow was falling; it was cold, sometimes very cold. We usually had eggs, toast and hot coffee or cocoa. The owner had a new machine. He said, "Boys, you have never seen a thing like this before, not even in Europe." At the counter he had a glass box which he opened and put some eggs in. Then, presto, in seconds the eggs were ready to eat. It was one of the first microwave ovens in Philadelphia. Then we would start to work. My paper boss drove a huge station wagon full of Sunday newspapers and I, sitting in the back, had to fold them together and with some skill I learned to throw them at the door of our customers. That was the real job. I sometimes had to run after the car while watching my business too. Sometimes I slipped on the steps and the heavy paper bundle fell apart in the bushes. That was not good, but I learned to do it like a real Philadelphia paper boy.

One day one of my neighbors stood behind his curtains and shouted to me on the street, "You hungry guy, you hungry guy!" I didn't know what a hungry guy was. I had just had a good breakfast with two eggs and toast and I wasn't hungry at all. But then my driver explained that the neighbor just didn't like for me to make too much money. At that job I earned about $90, and for that money we bought a used piano and then had music in the house.

There were other things hard to understand. For example, a 'closet' in English is a cabinet, in German it is a toilet. A 'hot dog' in English is a sausage, in German it is a warm street mutt. Or a 'gift' store in English is a souvenir shop, but in German the word 'gift' means poison. And there were many more language challenges to learn.

Then came another great event in our daily life. My brother-in-law would come to America too. He had three boys and when we departed from Bremerhaven, Germany, he had stood on the pier looking up at us on the boat going away to our dreamland America. He wanted to go with us and I thought he would almost jump into the water and try to join us. He too had had a hard time, sometimes working eighty hours a week just to break even with all the daily expenses. Life was hard in the big cities of Germany and for many the promise of America was the only solution. We promised him that when we were doing better that we would help him to come over to our paradise. Things began to work out pretty good for him. At our German church we had a bakery owner who agreed to sponsor him and promised to give him a job in the bakery. To our surprise, after only six months he too was ready to sail from Germany to New York.

Now we had to look for an apartment for him in our neighborhood. It was not easy to find because no landlord wanted to rent to a family with three boys. After days of looking we found an older lady who was willing to help. We collected some furniture and other things and our good minister picked them up at the harbor in New York. What a joy to have some of our own flesh and blood with us in Philadelphia! We packed all the kids one after another into one room and the parents into the other room. But the small place was only temporary and we soon found another larger apartment in the same neighborhood. But, to our surprise and horror, they found that the whole house was full of cockroaches; small and large ones all over the place. You didn't see them in the daytime, but at night the whole house came to life. All the kitchen cabinets were full of them, as were the beds and everything else. What should they do, move again? We all helped in fighting these little beasts. First we put the bedsteads in kerosene cans, then cleaned the kitchen as best we could and back to house hunting. Here in America we learned you could buy a house without money, and we did. With borrowed money the new family moved into the first house of their own—without any roaches but a thirty year mortgage. Now life was getting better, but was still not perfect. So the brother-in-law, Willi, bought a used car, a 1949 Plymouth and life on the fast track began.

To get away from my Polish dance party every weekend I started house hunting too. With the realtor I drove around the city until he found something he wanted to sell me. The price was too high for me so I told him, "I don't want to get into debt." But the realtor only laughed.

"Mr. Haas, why not?" he asked. "When you are in debt you will work better."

But this was not my idea of needing to work. By driving around some more I found a house that I liked, but the realtor told me it was not offered through his company. In the evening I went to the owner of the house accompanied by an older lady we'd met who knew the realty business and after checking the house she suggested, "It is a good house and I will give you a loan with easy interest, only 3½%, if that is all right with you?"

Then, with another realtor, I bought the house for $8,500. It had three bedrooms upstairs, a kitchen, living room, dining room, huge basement and garden space in front and back. My, what more would I need? I had to pay 20% down, and that was just what I had saved over time; the rest would be from the bank loan. I was surprised that the bank would loan me the money. In Germany it would never have happened. Loaning money to a stranger with no security? But the realtor only laughed and said, "Why not? In the bank the money does no good. Don't you know why the dollar is round? It has to move. You are a German with a good profession and good job, you are a healthy family so why not? Take this house and be happy."

He was right. Now I was a happy homeowner and my American dream had become a reality.

In order to finish the purchase business I had to go to the title company and so needed some time off from my job. The next day I asked Frank about it. "Why do you need time off?" Frank asked. I told him the story of my new house and how I had to go to the title company. He was surprised. "What, you are buying a house? You have only been in this country for two years. It took me ten years to buy my first house here. Where did you get the money?" When I told him the story he just shook his head. "You German guy, you can do miracles, but I wish you good luck."

But then, even in this fine northern Philadelphia home, there was the surprise waiting for me again. In the basement I discovered we had Chinese roaches. We lived in a duplex and I asked the next door lady about them. She said, "You will get used to them. They are only in the basement and around the furnace, they'll do you no harm." But I didn't like those guys. I bought some poison spray and worked with it in the basement and, oh wonder, the roaches disappeared in a short time. I was winning the war.

One day I told Mrs. McCarty, "See, my roaches are all gone, gone like the wind."

"What did you do?" she asked.

"Oh, it wasn't much; I just used some poison spray and now they have disappeared." I told her.

She looked at me, "Disappeared? You rascal, now I know where all the new roaches in my basement came from. You sent them over to me. Stop that. You just sent them to me; stop that or I will spray too and send all those guys right back to you again." I stopped spraying, but I bought some cement and closed all the cracks and holes around the back yard and at last killed them. After that I had peace from those little beasts.

Some time later two strangers knocked at my door and wished to speak to me. I was busy hanging wallpaper in the living room, but when they spoke in my German language I let them in. "Hey, mister, you're working so hard, don't you know we will not live forever? Too many of you newcomers from abroad just work themselves to death and then what? You should take care of the important things first, don't you know?"

"No, these walls need to be fixed and I don't like to live in a shack," I explained.

They laughed. "You are right, but there are so many more important things in life." Every Sunday evening they held evangelistic meetings. Wednesday was prayer meeting, Friday was Bible study. On the weekends there was worship and other events as well as church business meetings. Besides that they went around the neighborhoods three or four evenings from 6:00 to 9:30 PM, collecting money for the new church building. The minister was never burned-out in his service for the Lord. This also included picnics and outdoor meetings which he even filmed for the later indoor entertainment of the church.

That summer we all went to a camp meeting in the beautiful Pennsylvania countryside. What is America without knowing and experiencing a real camp meeting? You have to be there; you will never forget it.

When we went the first time with our good pastor I thought I was back in the time of old Israel in the desert. It was almost a tent city in the open farmland, surrounding a very big tent which had room for about 2,000 people. There were real streets among the tents and our family lived there for the whole week. You have to see this, especially for the first time. It was a total surprise for me in our modern world. But all the people enjoyed the togetherness the entire time, attending meeting after meeting of all the different religious education for all ages.

Attending the large meetings in the huge tent it was hard for me to understand everything that was being said. Many times the preacher was really spontaneous and the people were too. There were about two thousand people there and I was right in the middle of it all. It was often very exciting. When the preacher made a good point, right beside me a woman would suddenly jump up and shout, "Hallelujah, Hallelujah," waiving both arms high in the air. Then another shout came from another corner, "Amen, Amen!" What was going on? Then another shout came from behind me, "Brother, you are right! Praise the Lord!" Others did the same. I thought, my, you would never see things like this in Germany. No listener would ever dare to interrupt the sermon of the pastor, but here it sounded like everybody belonged to the great Tent Family. There was too much warm air in the tent and too many little bugs flew around. So all of these two thousand people waved paper fans with a picture of Jesus on them to cool themselves. That was really funny, seeing those two thousand Jesus pictures waving around during the sermon. What an idea! But this too was America even though it was really strange for me. Because I was looking around to see what was happening I couldn't follow the sermon of the preacher very well and my mind wandered. This noisy meeting would never have happened in Germany, or would it?

Suddenly I remembered a noisy religious meeting in my hometown of Mainz. It was about 1937, or so. At that time there was a big fight in Germany about the new Christian religion. The strong Nazi party wanted one thing and the Protestant Church wanted another. There was a big meeting in our town hall about the planned new Deutsche Kirche (Church) supported by the new government. The regular Protestant Church didn't like that idea and on this evening about four thousand people filled the large arena listening to various preachers. To our shock, there was a big noise from the back of the hall and about thirty storm troopers pushed forward toward the platform. They wanted to talk also. They wanted to gain the platform but the people tried to push them out of the room. Then these men started singing the once famous song Die Fahne Hoch (High the Flag), making even more noise. The ministers on the platform began praying the Lord's Prayer. The Nazi's sang louder but the ministers prayed louder too. Then all the four thousand people in the room including my sister and me prayed too, "Our Father, which art in Heaven . . ." It was an unforgettable evening. The Nazis were singing louder and louder and we did the same with our prayers. In the midst of the tumult someone had called the police and they arrived and cleared out the hall, ending the meeting. On our way home my sister said, "This was a great event, almost history. You will see, the Nazis will not win." But then they did.

Back at camp meeting I learned that for many people this was the only vacation they would have the whole year long. By participating in these things we grew more and more into the American way of life and we liked it. Our so-called German church didn't have many real German members; most came from other parts of Europe: Ukraine, Slovakia, Poland, Hungary or Austria, so mainly our language held us together along with our religion. We taught the children the German language and for good reason. We still had many relatives back in Germany and how would the kids be able to speak with their Oma if they didn't know the language? So we all tried to learn in our spare time—the adults, English and the kids, German.

On rainy days we went to many of the famous museums in Philadelphia. I had come from a town that also had a great historical background. Mainz celebrated its 2,000th year anniversary. I was invited by the city fathers, but I could not go because I needed the money for my house and now we wanted to learn about American history. Philadelphia was rich in history and we were always discovering something new and interesting. Valley Forge, with the old Hessian names on the grave stones let us know what people had done for the new country and the new freedom they enjoyed so much. We visited the Delaware River crossing site by George Washington and on Sunday friends took us to Atlantic City. This was a great event. To stroll along the wide boardwalk by the ocean, it was unforgettable. Then we went to Longwood Garden and we also discovered the "Coca Cola Lake" in New Jersey and had fun. (Swimming in this brown lake in New Jersey, Gerhard said, "This is like swimming in Coca Cola, and so it was for us the Coca Cola Lake.) And one of the best things we learned about the lake was eating ice cream on the way back home.

A very special day was a tour to Washington, D.C. It turned out to be a great trip. The whole morning we walked around the big city and the famous places until we came to the Capitol. My, that was a building! We followed a tour guide into the big Senate room, listening to all the historical explanations from the guide, when, right in the middle of the talk Gerhard said, "Daddy, Daddy, look, here are Nazis all over."

I said, "Will you be quiet! Don't talk nonsense. What is in your head? This is the American Capitol, there are no Nazis, they are all gone."

But Gerhard started again with his Nazis, "See Daddy, here are the Nazis, all over on the chairs of the senators."

"Will you be quiet! They will arrest us right here." But then I was curious about our talk and I looked at the chairs of the senators. There, woven right into the seats of the chairs I could see the sign of the Nazis, the Swastika. I could not believe my eyes, but it was true.

How could this have happened? Then Gerhard was quiet and later I had to explain to him about this old heathen symbol of the sun used by the Greeks and other nations of old times. It had nothing to do with the Nazis; they just discovered the sun symbol for their emblem two thousand years later. Surprising what children can see and remember.

One day one of my friends said, "Kurt, it's time you bought a car of your own. We've driven you around long enough with your family and we all have a good time. We did the same thing a long time ago." That was a big event in my life, buying a car in America. My brother-in-law sold me his old 1949 Plymouth for $75 and taught me to drive the stick shift. I thought I would never learn, but he was persistent. Then I had to get my driver's license. My, I would be alone in the car only with the policeman beside me. But I made it after all and now I was alone on the road. That was something for me. Sitting there behind the wheel, all the other cars seemed to come straight toward me. But I just held to my line—what a blessing that there was a white line on the road. My, I did it and it was great! I could drive all alone through the streets of Philadelphia, even beside the street cars and other traffic. What a success. The next week I came home in the evening and wanted to park right in front of my house. But there was another car there and I got my foot mixed up and went straight up the driveway toward the front door. The motor died and what was I to do? Nobody was around, so as fast as I could I started it again, shifted into reverse and oh, wonder, the car backed out and parked right beside the other car. Nothing happened and I was saved.

Another time I was late to work. I wanted to pass an oil truck; the car in front of me did it and I followed right behind him. But when I was along side the oil truck, another car came straight toward me. What to do? I had nowhere to go and I could see myself already crushed to pieces. But the oncoming car went over the front lawn of the nearby house so I pushed the gas pedal down and flew over to the right side with my car still in control. I was saved, but never did this again. Trying to pass without seeing exactly the other side—no more. There is still lots of learning until you are really in control of your driving business.

My sister wanted to come from Germany and I wanted to pick her up with my old car at New York Harbor. My brother-in-law didn't like that idea, so he told my wife, "When he goes with this old car to New York he will be stuck in the Holland Tunnel. There will be a hundred cars in front of him and a hundred cars behind and all the huge trucks around; what will he do? And when he comes out on the other side in Manhattan and runs into the traffic of New York, it will be a catastrophe."

I said, "What catastrophe? The Philadelphia police gave me the driver's license; I drive all around the city and in the four weeks of driving I've never had an accident, you will see, everything will go well." So we left early to cross the Palmyra Bridge into New Jersey and then drove toward New York. When I saw the great dark hole I knew it was the Holland Tunnel. There was no other way, I went straight in and kept on driving.

Willi was right. There were hundreds of cars in front and behind me plus huge trucks. And the noise! It was a terrible thundering rumbling all around. Then Gertrud shouted, "Will you please close the window!" I did and it was much quieter in the car. Now we could even talk together. The tunnel seemed almost endless, but after a while we came out on the streets of New York. To our surprise there was not much more traffic than in old Philadelphia. We reached the harbor, picked up my sister from the boat and went back through the big city toward the huge George Washington Bridge. What a drive. From about ten lanes we went into the right one easily. I just kept in my lane like everybody else and we made it pretty good.

Then Gerhard shouted, "Daddy we made it! Now we are in New Jersey and Uncle Willi was wrong."

"Yes, we made it. We went through the Holland Tunnel under the Hudson River like a submarine and now we are over the George Washington Bridge and nothing happened. What will Uncle Willi say?" I asked.

At home he didn't say much, just, "There must have been a good angel with you."

The wife of one of our neighbors was from Vienna, and sometimes another man from Vienna, a visitor, came into this house. It was Eugene Ormandy, the well-known conductor of the famous Philadelphia Symphony Orchestra. There I was introduced to the Philadelphia summer concerts at the Robin Hood Dell in the vicinity of Fairmont Park. This was something special. To sit in this open air theater, surrounded by about 20,000 people, listening to professionally played classical music has been unforgettable. It was fantastic. To see all the many music lovers ready to watch the famous conductors, this was also America. The shouting of the many popcorn vendors and all the noise in the area stopped when the conductor raised his baton high in the air. Gerhard was excited. "Daddy, someday I will play also in this great Robin Hood Dell Orchestra."

But Erika just said, "Daddy, look, all the stars above and there goes an airplane right over the orchestra." It was great—listening to the classical music in the outdoor evening atmosphere was a delight. The Philadelphia nights were so warm and easy going, you could feel the warmth and might catch the flying lightning bugs in front of you. When we came back home we would sit in our porch swing. Why should we go to bed so early? We had no air conditioning and the bedrooms were as warm as saunas. We didn't need covers and it was amazing how the human body adjusted to the different surroundings and climates.

Then I began to make my big mistake. I changed my work place and did something new. I met an Austrian fellow who was looking for a good foreman in his factory. We spoke the same language and this made it easier for him to become acquainted with me. "Kurt," he said, "come over with me and you will easily make $20 more a week." At that time $20 was good money. "You have been in your old store long enough, it's time to do something new. We have 250 people working in our plant and we need some experts. Talk it over with your boss, this will be your opportunity."

Now I had been about three and a half years at my old job, so why not make this change? America is the land of ambitious people; there will always be something better. The next day I had a talk with Frank, my boss in the store. From the beginning Frank didn't like my idea. "Did you ever work in a factory? You didn't, you don't really know what it is you will run into. It's very different from the work you are doing now and have done in the past. You are a very fine custom tailor, you are not a factory man. Working at a machine you become like the machine itself." But in the end I only saw the $20 more on the Friday evening when I would get my check so I quit my job at the fine store, went over to the factory and was hired as a foreman. But, to be a foreman you have to know all the positions of the workers under you. I knew them by theory, but in practice it is something different and here it was really something else. Totally new machines, new material, new time conditions and people. To be equal with my workers or above them, at least I had to finish the work pieces like they did. Otherwise I wouldn't make the $20 more per week. Now I knew what factory work was and what the people had to do to make more money than at my old place. To be equal I had to finish about 100 pieces every day at my position. I never did it. If you lose one minute's time in the morning it will always increase to more toward the evening and you will never make up the time or the work or the money. When I came home after a few days of my new work, I had to lay down on the sofa, exhausted and almost shaking like a man with palsy. The next day, the same thing—just driving myself to stay up with my coworkers and their work. The people beside me had the same situations, we all had to finish our daily quotas.

The lady across from me put an alarm clock on the machine right in front of her eyes, always watching the minutes going by and the work with her hand on the machine. The man beside me was a very fast worker—he even had time to watch me in my struggle to keep up. After some time he said, "Kurt, you have to do something different or you will never catch up. Do what I do. You know what I do? I pray to Mary and you have to do the same thing. You have to pray to Mary. You will learn that Mary will help you too. You have to say, and he shouted it, 'Mary, Mary help!' and you know what, Mary is always there, she will help you too." Then he finished his cigarette and with shaking hands kept on working hard, racing with the machine and the time.

On my left side was Peter, working at the same position I had. In time I noticed something strange. He never worked on Monday. Why? I asked him about it and he said, "Kurt, you know I am not young any more. I still have five years to go until my retirement from this place. It is not easy for me. On Saturdays I have to see the doctor and on Mondays I have to rest from my hectic work of the week before. What you are doing in five days I have to do in four otherwise I won't make it." With shaking hand he kept on pushing the work under the machine. Even at lunchtime he used his time off to get prepared for the afternoon run.

The whole factory floor, with all the running noisy machines and the shouting people looked to me like a real mad house. From the ceiling blared the radio music all around us and the Italian ladies sang opera in all tones. Then abruptly the power went out—silence—nobody could work. It happened very often because of all the power cables running over the floor and around the machines. It wouldn't have been so bad, but the time we lost in our work was also money we lost Friday on payday. At the end of the seventh week I had enough of it and I quit. The boss didn't like it. He said, "Kurt, only a few more weeks and you will make it, don't go into another place." But I left and went back to Frank at my old place.

Now Frank said, "Didn't I tell you before? Didn't I tell you not to go into the factory? But now I have no work for you. I hired another man when you left and I can't let him go so fast. Now you have to find another job. The city is big and you will find one; good luck."

Now I was job hunting again after three and a half years. I was out of the good store. But Philadelphia was a great industrial city with many places for a job seeking man and I found one very quickly. Nearby my area was a branch store of the finest department store in Philadelphia, John Wanamaker. The next morning I went to see the foreman. I always did this, that is, saw the foreman first. Usually the foreman knows better about the work situation than the office people. And he was busy, he just needed a man like me to finish the daily work. When I told him my story (I found out he was also a German), he hired me on the spot. I should come the next day and when I started to go a man from the back of the huge workroom shouted, "Don't hire this Nazi, we don't need Nazis in our store!"

When I looked in his direction I saw a black man at the pressing machine who worked with me in another store. I went straight to him, "Bob, what's the matter with you? You know I am not a Nazi, why all this shouting?"

"Yeah, what's the matter? You just come into the room and in a split second you are hired, you are just like the other guy, you are all Nazis," he insisted.

"Bob, did you ever see a Nazi? If you want this new job yourself I'll give it to you, but I am not the foreman. I'll find another job somewhere. We white people are not better than you black ones, we are just different and it is not our fault, that's all." I said.

"Yeah, don't you know we all came from the same dirt. Why are you always treated better? You are still a Nazi anyway," he said.

"Bob, how do you know I'm a Nazi?" I asked.

"Very easy," he replied. "You are a German and all Germans are Nazis." I almost laughed at this answer, but what should I say? How could you explain to a simple man who had never been outside the country the complex system of the former Nazi dictator?

Then I asked, "Bob, would you like to see my papers? I could never come into this country if I were a Nazi."

"Yeah, papers; what papers? You are a German, so you are a Nazi, that's all." he concluded. What should I say? We were worlds apart in many ways, but later when we worked together again there was no difference between black and white. We even became good friends and that's the way it should be, and this is America also.

At this place we had a new mysterious problem. Every week the sales people missed some of their merchandise. The camera department, the jewelry department and others around could not explain where the stuff went. Who did the stealing, if that was what it was? The store tried all the tricks, even called the police, but things continued to disappear. What was going on here? When we left the store we were all checked but nothing was found. We had a good night watchman making the rounds all night and he found nothing. Then one day a customer found a new camera from our store beside the flag pole in the bushes. The only person who raised the flag each morning was the night watchman and he was thought to be a very honest fellow, but the next morning one of our security men was hiding in the bushes beside the pole. Then it happened. The night watchman came out of the store with the flag rolled like a bundle, went straight into the bushes and came back to raise the flag as usual. And in the bushes was all the missing stuff. Now the man waited and a little later a car drove up. The driver got out, went to the bushes and collected all the stolen stuff and drove away. That was good teamwork, but the next day they were both arrested. We hired a new night watchman and the stealing stopped. What a funny trick to play with Old Glory of America; to steal with the help of our American flag just to make a few dollars the wrong way. But this happened not only in America, it happened all over the world. All the time people lose their connection with God's Ten Commandments.

The Wanamaker store was not only the finest in Philadelphia, it was Philadelphia itself. This store was so big it occupied a whole city block; twelve stories high and the basement the same size. The subway went right into it and in bad weather we had the best business. Going shopping was just a delight, strolling around all the departments and listening to the huge organ from the fifth floor. This was something. In the middle of the entrance was plenty of room to browse around. You could buy all kinds of things and listen to great music from Bach, Beethoven or Bruckner while still having a great time buying shoes, perfume or shaving cream.

And there was the great Eagle, a romantic spot for rendezvous for all kinds of people. It was the meeting point for many during the lunch time and it was a famous place in the city.

To come to my new work place, which was a new branch of the Wanemaker's store in the suburbs, I had to use my own car and forget riding the subway downtown. In some ways I missed the riding excitement. There had always been interesting people to meet and unexpected happenings. Like sudden strikes, some with strange surprises. On my way home one day the train driver stopped, left his seat and proceeded to leave the train. "Folks, we are on strike, you have to walk home," he announced.

He wanted to leave the car, but a very tall heavy man stood up. "Folks, you are not walking home, you all came here and if the driver doesn't bring the train to our place, this will be his last ride." He commanded the man, "You! You get back into the seat and take us to the end station, or, this is the last time for you on this subway." We all stood up and went to the front of the car, surrounding the driver. He looked at us, then turned around, started the car and on we went to the last station. Then we all shouted, "Thank you, good boy!" The strike was over.

Another time I was not so lucky. I went home on the train very late, about 10:00 PM, and I had to switch to the bus. The bus to my street was late and it was a lonely corner behind a business section, but now totally dead. Nobody was around and I waited in the dark. Across from my bus stop was a bar or tap room with a jolly noisy crowd. The door opened and a lady, totally drunk came out and came over to my side of the street. She then discovered me, shouting, "Jimmy, Jimmy, where have you been?" She tried to give me a big hug and kiss me. "Oh, Jimmy, come kiss me, you are my best friend, don't you know?" She smelled like alcohol and I had a hard time to push her away from me. Then the door opened again and two heavy set men came out, also drunk and reeling from one side of the sidewalk to the other.

Then they discovered the woman at my side, "Mary Louise, what are you doing with this white man? Wait, we'll come and finish him off; wait a minute." They tried to run over to me but they were so drunk they had a hard time staying on their feet. Then my bus came. With all my strength I struggled free from Mary Louise and ran to the bus. It was high time, now the three ran after the bus trying to catch me. The driver said, "Boy, you are lucky, you would have had no chance to get away. Where have you been?"

Now, to drive my car to work was new and different too, especially in wintertime. When we had a blizzard the whole city was dead. The cars on the street were snowed-in, the city snowplows came out at night and pushed the snow right in front of the wheels which then froze to ice. I had to hack the car out of the ice with a screw driver. I broke the ice in the radiator, poured in a little warm water and started the car.

It was hard to warm the car up and it always took too long to do. I had to think of some other way. I remembered my father in Germany had warmed a car by putting a cardboard in front of the motor and then it started easier. I thought I'd do the same thing. I opened the hood, put some newspapers around the inside and gave the car a test drive before going to work. I went around the block and suddenly I saw blue smoke coming out of the motor in front. I got scared, stopped the car and lifted the hood. A huge blue-gray cloud came out of the car. All the paper smelled like it was burning. I grabbed all the paper and threw it into the snow. I was saved. Across the street a service station attendant was watching. "You crazy boy," he shouted, "you can't do this with modern cars, you could blow it up and be burned up in no time." It was my last car warming—I didn't do that any more.

Citizenship

Now we had lived almost five years in the United States and it was time to become real citizens. Many immigrants didn't think this way. Some only wanted to make enough money and then go back home where they came from. Others didn't like the kind of work or the manner of living here. They always thought it should be here like it was in the old country. In the beginning I sometimes thought this way too until my boss told me, "Kurt, you have to be flexible in America, otherwise you will never make it." So this was the way I learned.

But another man I knew just went home with his whole family. But after just a few months he came back. When back in Germany at his old place he tried to introduce the new American way of working. But the fellows there said, "No way, you work like we do or go back to America." So he came back. Others were always homesick until they went home to the old place and saw it wasn't the same any more and decided America was the best place after all.

I thought, I am making my money here; I came here to stay and educate my kids for a better life than I had in the old country and now, now it is the time to take out citizenship. We made all the necessary applications and took seminars in American history and government. We polished our English and when the time came we handed all the paperwork into the office and waited. Later we took some tests and then came the date to be sworn in.

It was a glorious day in Philadelphia. All together there were over a hundred people to be sworn in sitting right in front of the old Independence Hall. People from all over Europe and elsewhere wanted to become members of a new nation in just the short time of five years of good living here. Then we would be real Americans. What a sensation; what a new beginning in a new country. At the right side, the statue of old George Washington watched us, in front was the Liberty Bell inside the historic hall, and on a huge high and fancy decorated stage was the whole Pennsylvania Supreme Court. To the left of them were the colorful uniforms and flags of the Valley Forge Military Academy and Boy Scouts of America color guards. An interesting program followed with good speeches by high ranking men. One speech I will always remember. It was the address by one of the high judges of the court.

He said, "New citizens, you new citizens of America, never forget to love your old country where you came from. We all came from abroad, some a long time ago, but these are our roots and from these lands you and all of the former immigrants who came to the shore of America have brought many talents and much knowledge into this land of ours. If you cannot love your old country which educated you and gave you life, how will you love this new country in which you are still new? Never forget your old roots while you never stop improving your new life here."

When all the naturalization ceremonies, including the first proclamation of Law Day in the USA was over, we all felt hungry. No wonder, it had started at 10:00 AM and lasted to 1:00 PM. We strolled over to Market Street, looking for a good restaurant. There was none better than John Wanamaker's Fifth Floor restaurant. We were all dressed up and when the waiter came asking for our wishes, he was really surprised by just looking at us. "Folks, what's the occasion? Why on a Monday at noon are you so dressed up?" he asked.

Then Gerhard said, "Oh, today we are new citizens of America, can't you see it?"

The waiter laughed, "So, that's the big occasion. This has to be celebrated for sure. What will you eat?" When we hesitated about the menu he said in a jolly voice, "We have for this occasion Chicken a la King, that's what you should all eat today. You must feel like a king when you have just become

U.S. citizens, don't you think so?" We said, yes, and enjoyed the food and the jolly waiter and had a good time at the fine restaurant. We later strolled around in our good suits and festive dresses until evening in old Philadelphia. The day was too short. It was a great day and one of the best in our life.

The next day in our store everybody knew now that I was a new American, but Bob shouted across the workroom, "You were not born here, if you don't behave you will be shipped back to where you came from."

Then the foreman said, "He knows more about the country than you who were born in the USA, leave him in peace, the war is over."

Later the foreman asked me what I did in the war and if I was in a POW camp. He himself did not go to Europe or any other front; he did his duty in Philadelphia where he watched German POWs in camps. When I told him I was some time in a USA POW camp he said, "Kurt, when you were in the US camp, you must have had it better than back home with your father and mother in the old Fatherland. We gave the men a good time, better than ever until the war ended. This we always did."

I said, "Sam, it was different than at home with father and mother and I am glad it is over." Then I told him about my time at Steyr in Austria in the camp. "I was glad it was not so long and after eight weeks I was sent home, otherwise I was not sure if I would make it. I was already hungry the day when I entered the camp site. The first five days I had nothing to eat and then the food business became organized. Too many soldiers laid around by the river Enns under the trees in the meadow. It was still very cool at night and where I was the rain started. We had nothing to cover us and got wet as dogs. In the morning all our clothes and underwear were drenched with water. We got permission to make a fire and took off all our clothes and by sitting around the fire naked we waited for the clothes to dry to put them on again. This happened many times. I was lucky; we had a good well by the river and we drank water all the time to fill our empty stomachs. But I was still hungry. I wanted to make some soup. I collected different grasses, put them in a tin can with water and cooked it over our fire. After drinking the new vegetable soup, I became so sick I almost died. I didn't do that any more and waited for better food. Then it came. At 6:00 in the morning a truck from the headquarters kitchen brought us one cup of black water, so-called coffee. At noon the truck came again with lunch and dinner in one operation. For twelve men we had one can of sardines in oil. There were six sardines in the one can. Everybody got half a sardine and one slice of bread. We ate it right away so nobody could steal it. For one piece of bread the soldiers gave up wedding rings or watches just to have something to eat. Then came my lucky hour.

"The next morning at 8:00, about 100 men were released and I was one of them. I could have jumped for joy. Free—free after all those long war years in Europe. We were loaded on open trucks like a bunch of cattle and driven to Germany. It took two days to drive there and I went to my uncle on a farm in middle Germany. I could not go home to my folks at the end of the war." I told him.

Sam asked, "Why couldn't you go home?"

"Sam," I explained, "there was no more home. While I was still in Italy at the end of February, 1945, my sister sent me a telegram and a newspaper report about the end of my home town. I still have it and I will translate it for you so you can read it tomorrow." This I did and then brought him the report of this historic day in WWII:

More than 1,000 Bombers over the city of Mainz

27th February, 1945—Our Hour of Horror

4:20—Full Alarm. Together with the terrible noise of the first sirens, the first exploding bombs also fell over the sleeping city. In a very fast action 4,000 tons of bombs, as falling from a burst sack, were poured down on all the houses. The first target was the oldest part of the city and in no time all the streets appeared like a burning sea of exploding phosphorus canisters—an endless firewall. The noise and cracking of the fast falling bombs was so terrifying and frightening for everybody around. The people out of their early sleep were running all over the streets for some kind of protection toward cellars or bunkers. But everything was too fast for them. In the middle of the burning streets they became a blaze of living torches, screaming and running for help and in their desperation felt like they were paralyzed. In a few minutes there was no way out of this hell fire. There was almost no air left and people suffocated right there on the streets. This deadly spectacle lasted only twenty-two minutes and then Mainz was no more.

Only a dark cloud, huge and endless covered the wide sky like a grandiose occurrence of nature. Those mammoth clouds filed the whole Rhine River valley and became bigger and bigger. In those clouds of dust and flying dirt was the whole city of Mainz. A city, with normally 100,000 inhabitants and with a 2,000 year history, was dead. Everything was pulverized and burned like it only could happen in real hell fire itself. After twenty-two minutes this city was a city of the dead.

I told Sam, "My sister and other people crawled out of the rubbish of the burning houses, running toward the Rhine banks for fresh air and cooling. They used the water of the cool Rhine and looked at their city. The fire was five kilometers long along the river bank making the shining water look like blood. There they waited for the end of the day, or the end of the war or the end of the world. Whatever came first, it made no difference. This inferno ordeal made no sense."

Then Sam said slowly, "Kurt, it was war, but aren't you glad it's all over? Now you should forget, now you will have it better."

"Yes, Sam, if you hadn't asked me I would never have said it, I want to forget and I am very glad I am here now in your country. It is not Paradise, but for the moment it feels like it is and I hope it stays so."

Yes, I had nothing to complain about. I had a good job, Gertrud worked as a nurse in a nearby hospital and the two children were doing good in school. Gerhard learned to play his violin from Mr. Zapf at the conservatory, and Erika, she didn't like the piano, but she was good in school. My brother-in-law was a good conductor of our little church choir. Gertrud played the piano and I the new Hammond organ. It was a happy time for us immigrants in the new country. It had been a long and exiting way from the year 1945 in Germany to the year 1960 in Philadelphia.

When I was released from prison camp and was set free in middle Germany, one US soldier said to me, "Auf Wiedersehen." He and I didn't know fifteen years later that I and my whole family would become US citizens. The US Consul in Frankfurt was right. When I left he said, "Mr. Haas, if you obey our laws and if you adjust to the way of living over there in America, you will have all that you want now." So why would I make another different move?

But things went differently. Our Willi wanted to go to California. He didn't like the big city. He sold everything in Philadelphia, rented a U-Haul trailer and disappeared to California. He even wanted to take us with him, but why should I go? Why should I sell my nice place and move again into a new adventure? But, after a year I did the same thing. I too sold my house, rented a trailer and with all the leftover stuff traveled toward California. As a co-worker said to me, "Young man, go West." But this is another big story about "Why America?"

So far I could only say, Thank You America, and Thank God in heaven for all the blessings; the blessings of good health, the blessings of good work and the blessings of knowing good friends in this new country, without which we would never have made it.

And this is "Why America?"

www.ingramcontent.com/pod-product-compliance
Lightning Source LLC
Chambersburg PA
CBHW020238290526
45784CB00003B/1028